ADDITIONAL ACCLAIM FOR *SPEED IS LIFE*

"Bob Davis understands the value of speed, timing, and decisive action in today's digital world. In *Speed Is Life,* he shares his observations, insights, and lessons learned based on personal experience. Bob doesn't merely theorize, he offers sound business principles based on results."

—EDGAR BRONFMAN, JR.,
EXECUTIVE VICE CHAIRMAN, VIVENDI UNIVERSAL

"Davis is one of the very few who can keep up with the highest speeds of life and still be able to explain it all effectively for all those . . . [who are] slower."

—BARRY DILLER, CHAIRMAN AND CEO, USA NETWORKS, INC.

"*Speed Is Life* isn't just a playbook for other Internet companies—it's a bible on strategy and tactics for business leaders and managers whatever field they are in."

—DESH DESHPANDE, CHAIRMAN, SYCAMORE NETWORKS

Speed is life

Speed is life

Street Smart Lessons
From the Front Lines
of Business

Bob Davis

< FOUNDER OF LYCOS >

CURRENCY

DOUBLEDAY NEW YORK LONDON TORONTO SYDNEY AUCKLAND

A CURRENCY BOOK
PUBLISHED BY DOUBLEDAY
a division of Random House, Inc.
1540 Broadway
New York, New York 10036

CURRENCY and DOUBLEDAY are
trademarks of Doubleday,
a division of Random House, Inc.

Book design by Vertigo Design, NYC

Library of Congress Cataloging-in-Publication Data
Davis, Bob, 1956–
    Speed is life : the CEO of Lycos reveals his secrets to surviving and thriving on Internet
    time / Bob Davis.—1st ed.
        p. cm.
    Includes index.
        1. Davis, Bob, 1956– 2. Telecommunications engineers—United States—Biography.
    3. Executives—United States—Biography. 4. Lycos, Inc. I. Title.

    TK5102.56.D38 A3 2001
    025.04'092—dc21
    [B]

                                                                        2001017477

ISBN 0-385-50136-6
Copyright © 2001 by Robert J. Davis
All Rights Reserved
Printed in the United States of America
First Edition: May 2001
SPECIAL SALES
Currency Books are available at special discounts for bulk purchases for
sales promotions or premiums. Special editions, including personalized
covers, excerpts of existing books, and corporate imprints, can be created
in large quantities for special needs. For more information, write to
Special Market, Currency Books, 280 Park Avenue, 11th floor, New York, NY 10017,
or e-mail specialmarkets@randomhouse.com.

10 9 8 7 6 5 4 3 2 1

For Rita, Rian, Michelle, and Daniel

ACKNOWLEDGMENTS

THIS BOOK, the result of a lifetime of experiences, was only possible with the help of many people along the way. I begin with my wife of 20 years, Rita, who tirelessly helped me write, edit, and critique revision after revision. As with all else in life, her suggestions and comments became my foundation. Also, Brian, Michelle, Daniel, the loves of my life, each in their own way my inspiration, who selflessly allowed their dad to give so much of his time to the career that made this book possible.

This work is an extension of me and my career. As it relates to me, thanks to Jim and Marie, my parents, who in our brief time together shaped me for a lifetime. To my brothers Jim and Dick and sister Marilyn and their children, Kurt, Craig, Jeff, Erin, Kelly, Kara, and Katie for the love and devotion we share with each other. To Kip and Nan, Pat and Michelle, Dave and Bernadette, Tom and Mary, Pam and Tim, Chris and Michelle, Rich and Mary, and John and Bette for being such great friends. To Boston College High School for its commitment to making a better world for me and the thousands of students before and after.

As it relates to my career, I offer thanks to the many who gave me the break I needed: John Callanan and Jim O'Sullivan at GE, Tom Murphy and Dick Orlando at Wang, and Dan Nova at Lycos. To my assistant at Lycos, Heather Webb, and before her,

Bev Willson, for their unending support. And, of course, I am eternally grateful to all the wonderful employees of Lycos, past and present, who were there for our exciting ride that will forever change media as we know it,especially the team that I worked so closely with over the last years—John McMahon, Dave Peterson, Ron Sege, Jeff Bennett, Tom Guifoile, Jeff Snider, and Madeline Mooney, and others before them, such as Jan Horsfall, Sangam Pant, Bo Peabody, Mark Simmer, and Jeff Crown. I am appreciative to the members of our board of directors for their commitment to both me and the company, who, in addition, to Dan Nova included Jack Connors, Dick Sabot, and Peter Lund. And to Ted Philip, the man more responsible than I for the success Lycos has enjoyed.

Finally, I offer a special thanks to all that made this book itself possible. I start with Donna Carpenter, Maurice Coyle, and their associates at Wordworks, who so ably partnered with me in the manuscript's creation. Thanks also go out to all at Lycos, who assisted in the substantial research effort. And lastly, to those who are willing to share their stories for doing business in a world where speed is life: Ernie Allen, Dan Case, Hon. Paul Cellucci, Jack Connors, Desh Deshpande, Charles Conn, Richard Egan, Richard Freeland, Timothy Forbes, Leo Higdon, Jan Horsfall, Naveen Jain, Don Keough, Robert Kraft, Calvin Lui, Atushi Nishijo, Dan Nova, Kevin O'Connor, Ted Philip, Dick Sabot, Alan Schwartz, Thomas Stemberg, and Paul Tagliabue.

CONTENTS

Speed is life

Beginnings

1

Beginnings

bgcolor=#336699> </td></tr><table
<FORM ACTION=http://www.lycos.com/srch/
<INPUT TYPE=hidden NAME=
Search for:</td>
Search for:</td>
size=25> <input type=image src=http://a6
<td colspan=4><font size=1 /font></td></tr></table> <table cellpadding=2

MY INTRODUCTION TO TECHNOLOGY took place while I was a student at Northeastern University in Boston. The school offered a work-study program, which enabled me to apply for a sales-training job at IBM. I really wanted that job.

The interviewer had told me he'd call that evening before 6 P.M. to let me know if I'd been accepted. I waited at home for the phone to ring—and waited and waited. When it finally did, I leaped to answer it: Wrong number. It rang several more times, but it was never IBM at the end of the line.

I sat alone in the house, tremendously disappointed. I'll never forget how empty the place felt. Eventually, I just crawled into bed.

A little after midnight, the phone rang again. This time it was the recruiter, who, after apologizing for calling so late, offered me the job. As it turned out, salvation at midnight was a fitting start for my career in technology, which has been full of unexpected twists and turns.

At the time, I had no glimmer of where that midnight call would lead. But more than 20 years later, I've just sold Lycos, one of the world's busiest Internet portals, to Terra Networks, a subsidiary of the Spanish phone giant Telefónica, for nearly $6 billion. I was the founder, president, and chief executive officer of the company during its entire life, which was less than six years long. During that brief but heady period the company went from being the brainchild of a university scientist to one of the Internet's most powerful media franchises. Operating in almost 30 countries, the Lycos Network is now used by nearly half of all Web users.

In some industries six years may not be that long, but on the Internet it's a lifetime—literally: The medium is six years old. It's a medium where traditional business cycles have been compressed into days. Its relentless growth has transformed not just the soaring—and often crashing—dot.coms but also the titans of the old economy. Companies such as General Electric, General Motors, and Wal-Mart—who placed little value on the Internet as recently as two years ago, have now made it a top priority.

Why has just about every enterprise on the planet, from rug-weaving cooperatives in India to multinational powerhouses, embraced the Internet? Because it is one of the most powerful communications tools in human history. Yes, it has extraordinary reach, but its greatest strength is speed. The ability to cull and disseminate information in the click of a mouse. It's no exaggeration to say that on the Internet, speed is life.

In this book, I want to share my thoughts and insights captured from the front lines of the Internet—as it was, as it is, and as it will be. But the lessons I learned at Lycos apply, in part, to running a business in *any* environment. There's a tendency to separate companies into Internet and non-Internet, as if the two were totally different species. I think that's a mistake. Internet businesses have much to learn from traditional organizations—and vice versa. After all, the business of the Internet is business—a refrain you will hear me repeat. So while I will, of course, tell you the story of how Lycos struggled, found its footing, and ultimately succeeded beyond all my expectations, the principles I've managed and succeeded by apply to organizations of all sizes and types.

I want to help readers understand what distinguishes a good company from an also-ran, what best practices have emerged from the Web, and what Internet and traditional companies—clicks and mortar—can offer one another as we move into the twenty-first century. The Internet is the most significant business development since the Industrial Revolution began in the middle of the eighteenth century. In that revolution, machinery that enabled mass production changed the course of human enterprise and determined economic, political, and national power. The Internet Revolution is driven not by machines, but by information, but it, too, is determining which companies, and even which countries, will prevail in the centuries ahead.

Perhaps I should start by sharing a few details of my own story.

I was born on October 6, 1956, in Dorchester, Massachusetts, a working-class neighborhood that Richard Egan, founder and chairman of data-storage giant EMC, likes to call "the Brooklyn of Boston." As one of four children who grew up a long way from Boston's famous Beacon Hill Brahmins, I've always had respect for the people who do the world's hard work.

I began my education at St. Mark's, a Catholic elementary school, where I wasn't a very disciplined student. I was much more interested in playing halfball with my friends. Halfball is essentially inner-city baseball—no diamond necessary. A sawed down broom handle was our bat, and we used it to hit a rubber ball that had been cut in half. What might have looked like a vacant lot to a passerby was Fenway Park to us. When the weather got cold, we turned our attention to hockey, once again using our wits. Our rink was a local park that we flooded by opening a nearby fire hydrant. The New England cold quickly did the rest. I learned much playing sports on the streets of Dorchester: camaraderie, teamwork, competitiveness—the skills that make up the lifeblood of any business. I wouldn't trade my childhood for any other.

So my academic career started inauspiciously. I didn't really understand the importance of learning and was pretty slow to crack my schoolbooks. The result was predictable and consistent mediocrity. Further complicating my young life was the fact that the nuns who taught at St. Marks, committed and dedicated as they were, had some long memories. On my first day in the second grade, for example, Sister Mary Hallorian asked if I was Dickie Davis' brother.

"Yes, Sister," I proudly responded.

"Class, Dickie Davis was a wise guy," Sister Hallorian promptly announced. Then she put me across her knee, spanked me, and said, "This will be a lesson. Don't be a fresh kid like your brother."

Well, I may have been a slouch when it came to school but I was always a hustler when it came to earning a few dollars. When I was a 12-year-old Boy Scout, I clipped an advertisement from the back of *Boy's Life* that promised I could earn "Big Cash." I mailed in the form and received a package that heralded the start of a long sales career. For the next few months I sold both magazine subscriptions and flower seeds door-to-door, in front of supermarkets, outside church, and even to the nuns at St. Marks (I don't remember if Sister Hallorian bought any). In total, I earned about $30 for my efforts—and thought I had struck it rich.

Looking for a way to spend my newfound wealth, I convinced my parents to take our first family trip outside the state of Massachusctts. It was during the Vietnam War, and my sister Marilyn lived in Aurora, Colorado, where her husband was stationed in the U.S. Air Force. I'm the baby in my family by a full eight years and a trip to see my big sister was quite a thrill. We flew out—my first plane ride—and after a bit of sightseeing in Colorado, we all drove to California to visit my father's brother. It was an incredible journey with many stops along the way— including the Rocky Mountains, the Grand Canyon, and Disneyland. But what I remember and treasure most were the stories we told, the songs we sung, and the deep love and sense of family we shared. It turned out to be the last vacation we ever had.

Within days of our return, my 53-year-old mother went to bed complaining of indigestion. When I woke up in the morning, I was told that she had been taken to the hospital during the night. Two days later, she died of heart failure.

All of a sudden, our family began to shrink. Weeks after my mother's passing, we lost my uncle in California; over the next five years, more than a dozen of my relatives died. My siblings grew up and moved out. My father worked all day, and the house was too empty for a 14-year-old. My after-school routine was fairly predictable: I came home and spent the afternoon crying over the loss of my mother. Then, somewhere around 5:00, knowing my father would be home soon, I pulled myself together. In my adolescent machismo, I tried to ease his suffering by presenting myself as composed and adjusted.

My father was my inspiration. A man of impeccable integrity, he ingrained in me the sense of ethics and fairness that would later allow me to run a multibillion-dollar company and still get a good night' sleep. Watching him deal with my mother's death was very painful. To this day, that was undoubtedly the most difficult period in my life.

My savior from this pain, which quickly became my home away from home, was Boston College High School. Founded on the principles of scholarship, faith, and community service, BC High was led by Jesuit priests whose devout commitment to their students kept me grounded during a very trying time. They pushed me to work hard and gradually instilled that most powerful of educational tenets: a love of learning. With several hours of homework each night, I slowly transformed from a C average laggard to an enthusiastic A student.

The Jesuits, who study for years to obtain their credentials, created an ethos of discipline, determination, and success. Having literally dedicated their lives to the education of a new generation, the priests saw no alternative to hard work. Perhaps most inspiring was the sense of community that I discovered at BC High. No one was left out, and differences were celebrated. The culture in many schools, then and now, is one in which children are embarrassed by academic excellence, because it isn't "cool" to be smart. At BC High, it was definitely cool to be a scholar, but we were also taught that life is about balance. A straight A student with no social skills was as ill equipped for his future as a great athlete who couldn't pass math. Overall excellence was the creed, and we were made to feel confident that we could achieve it.

When it was time for college, my selection criteria were simple: I needed a school I could afford that was an easy commute from Dorchester. Northeastern University, in the center of Boston, became the obvious choice. It offered a five-year degree program in which semesters alternated between classroom studies and full-time work related to one's major.

The school's proximity to home allowed me to continue living with my father, who I felt needed me. One of his favorite pastimes was to sit at the kitchen table with a cold bottle of beer listening to a Red Sox game on the radio. It was from exactly this position that he announced in August 1977, "I'm going into the hospital tomorrow." I was the cook in our house, and he told me that after years of my pan-grilled steak and Shake-and-Bake chicken, he wanted to try a spot with better food. In fact, he wasn't quite sure what the medical problem was, but at his most recent physical, his doctor had found him to be slightly anemic.

The "slight anemia" turned out to be acute leukemia, from which my father never recovered. He spent 33 days in the hospital, and I spent every free minute with him. When I arrived on day 34, I found him agitated and almost incoherent. "Take me home, Bobby," he said, calling me by my childhood name. "Just get me out of here." That day the hospital called in a priest to perform his last rites. Only then did he realize how truly ill he was. "My God, Father, am I that sick?" he asked.

He died the next day, at the age of 63; less than a month before my twenty-first birthday.

My father's life savings, combined with his insurance, left his children with a $14,000 inheritance. My $3,500 share, although helpful, was well short of what I needed to finish college, heat the house, and keep food on the table. My plan from that day on was straightforward: I would take care of myself.

For the next several years, I worked any odd job I could find, often two or three at a time. I drove a truck delivering groceries, was a lifeguard, did legal research, and, for six years, worked in a supermarket.

None of these jobs prepared me for the Internet per se, but what I learned about the working world was invaluable: the discipline of sticking to a schedule, getting up motivated in the morning, and the importance of just plain showing up. All of this may have been good for my character, but none of the jobs were very interesting, so you can imagine my excitement when that IBM sales-training opportunity came along. I latched onto it as if it were a life preserver. And while it may not have saved my life, it certainly altered its course.

IBM was a whole new world to me. I thought of the job in terms of sales training, as computers weren't part of my career plans, but quickly found that I loved the work. It was challenging, and I was surrounded by people my own age who I could talk to about the art of selling and about our plans and dreams for the future. We were amazed and intrigued by computer technology, even if we didn't quite understand it. And we certainly had no inkling of its potential. But, we were all proud to be working for a company that was a true market leader, the star of the nascent computer revolution.

After graduating from Northeastern with a near perfect grade-point average, I wanted to continue working for IBM as a full-fledged salesperson. But I received a reality check from a marketing manager who sat me down and said, "You have a baby face. Until you age a little, you won't be credible selling computers. Why don't you become an IBM support engineer?" Stymied by a "problem" I wouldn't mind having now, and with no desire to abandon sales, my career at IBM ended before it began.

In November 1979, a want ad in the *Boston Globe* led me to

a job at General Electric. I was 22, and that's when my career really started. My job was to sell communications devices and high-speed printers. We sold the equipment in bulk to computer companies, who then bundled it with the computers they sold.

My first year at GE was a real struggle, but I hit my stride during my second year and eventually became the top salesperson in my division. But I was dissatisfied. I felt constrained by the company's bureaucracy, and was gripped by a new ambition: I wanted to run a company, and I didn't see any chance of it being General Electric.

At the same time, a new company was getting a lot of attention across the country and particularly in the Boston area. You couldn't pick up a newspaper without reading about the accomplishments of high-flying, Massachusetts-based Wang Laboratories, a leader in the burgeoning world of office automation. I decided it was the place I wanted to be. Now I just needed to get myself hired.

I had several interviews with Wang that went nowhere because of my limited technology background. Then, once again, BC High came to my rescue. Tom Murphy, who had worked as a salesman at IBM during my internship, was a fellow alumnus. He'd taken me under his wing at IBM and when he heard I wanted to work for Wang, a company he'd recently joined as a sales manager, he put in a good word, and I was hired. It was the beginning of an 11-year career at Wang.

In 1984, I became branch manager in charge of a ten-person sales staff in Worcester, Massachusetts. This was my first management job, and I had to make the challenging transition from being part of the team to being responsible for it. Initially, I had mixed emotions about my new responsibilities. While I still felt part of the camaraderie of the crew, I now had to stand a little apart. I had to lead my friends, and they had to listen. It was probably as challenging for them as it was for me.

Gradually, I learned how to manage, and found that I enjoyed it. Tom Murphy, who by this time had become a regional manager, had promoted me to this new role. A great motivator and communicator, Tom taught me much of what I know about managing people. I also made some lasting friends in Worcester, among them Bev Willson, who was my first assistant there and now, 17 years later, is at Lycos.

It was at Wang that I met the person most responsible for my career. Dan Nova, a brilliant businessman, great philanthropist, and dear friend was a salesman who left the company to attend Harvard Business School and then went into venture capital. He is the person who, 11 years later, hired me as the Lycos CEO.

Wang was a roller coaster. I joined the company in its heyday, and by the time I left, it had filed for bankruptcy protection. It was a sad time for all of us, but I learned a lot. For example, I had to lay off something close to 200 people. Though firing people is occasionally necessary, and every chief executive has to know how to do it properly, it's terribly destructive to the employee, particularly when he or she doesn't deserve it, as was the case at Wang. The company needed to reduce costs as it played out a losing hand. These employees hadn't failed the company, the company had failed them. The experience reinforced my dedication to winning; I never wanted to face that situation again.

I also learned a great deal by watching Wang's mistakes. Its managers didn't anticipate fundamental market changes. Failing to see the coming personal-computer revolution, Wang clung to minicomputers. It wasn't just Wang that erred; all the minicomputer companies—Data General, Prime, Digital—disappeared because they weren't prepared for the market's rapid evolution.

Toward the end of that tumultuous time, I was part of a team working under John Chambers, who is now the CEO of Cisco Systems, and one of the great leaders in business today. It was Chambers who promoted me into my first job that involved managing managers. My job interview took place as I drove him to the airport. He asked a lot of tough questions; most memorable was his focus on building and shaping a team. Chambers really understood how to motivate and challenge people, a lesson I've never forgotten.

I left Wang soon after it filed for bankruptcy and took a job with Cambex, a small data-storage company that sold memory for IBM mainframes. In the world of technology, I could not have found a more "old world" business, but, it became another important step in my career. As the vice president of sales, I was responsible for all aspects of the company's revenue production. I began to understand the demands an executive manager faced, particularly in interacting with other key operational aspects of a business. I also came to love the environment of a smaller company.

After two years at Cambex, I answered the phone one day and heard my old pal Dan Nova's voice. He had recently joined a small venture-capital firm—CMGI—that was investing solely in the emerging Internet.

Dan told me that a new technology had come to his attention. It was a search engine called Lycos, derived from *lycosadae*, the Latin name for the wolf spider. In the Web's early days, the generic term for a search engine—automated software that roamed from Web site to Web site, creating an index of everything it passed—was a spider. It was enabled anytime a Web user typed in a word or phrase. The software would search the database built by the spider, then refer the user to all relevant Web sites. The Web's early spiders required so much computer-processing power that they could only operate at night when most of the computers they were indexing were idle. A wolf spider is nocturnal and, instead of waiting passively for something to fall into its web, it hunts its prey. The inventor shortened *lycosadae* to Lycos and the name was born.

Nova said that he was in the final stages of procuring a perpetual and exclusive license for the technology, and then planned to build a company around it. If the deal went through, CMGI would have to find a chief executive for Lycos.

"What about me?" I asked.

Dan didn't leap at the idea. He hemmed and hawed—saying no to a friend wasn't easy.

"What do you know about the Internet?" he asked.

"Absolutely nothing," was my honest answer.

"That might be a problem," he replied.

I assured him that I could and would learn.

The next day I subscribed to Prodigy, not realizing that, like America Online, it was, at that time, primarily a proprietary or closed service. When you were online with Prodigy you were pretty much limited to its self-contained content. When I told Dan about my Prodigy Internet account, he said, "You're just showing me how little you know." Nonetheless, he agreed to sit down and explain the technology and, during the course of that meeting, became supportive of my cause.

There was just one small problem: Lycos, as a company, didn't exist. It was a new technology that CMGI didn't even own yet. My heart was set on a job that wasn't real and might never be.

Lycos was the brainchild of Dr. Michael Mauldin, a computer scientist nicknamed Fuzzy, who had developed the technology at Carnegie Mellon. He knew he had a powerful invention and through the university's technology transfer office was attempting to commercialize his product. Mauldin was a researcher at heart and had no desire to go into business, not even with his own discovery. Moreover, the university didn't want to lose him.

I went down to Pittsburgh to meet Fuzzy. With his curly hair and a beard that camouflaged a large part of his face, Mauldin was almost a caricature of a scientist. I asked him how he had earned the nickname, assuming it was related to fuzzy logic. He politely responded, "Because I look that way." I immediately liked this intelligent and modest man, who was completely removed from the buttoned-down business world.

I returned to Boston and sat down to write a business plan for a company that might actually come to life someday. I spent a long and intense week projecting and shaping what Lycos might become. After I finished, I mailed it off to Dan Nova.

In the end, my grit and determination paid off. After a series of interviews with CMGI and at Carnegie Mellon, I was offered the job. Suddenly, I was, in June 1995, the CEO of a company based on a largely untested technology in an industry that no one really understood.

Over the next five-and-a-half years, I found myself in the thick of a historic revolution in communications, information, and human enterprise.

Speed is life

2

NOT LONG AGO, I was invited to tour a number of U.S. military facilities as a guest of William Cohen, then Secretary of Defense. The purpose of my visits was to gain firsthand knowledge of how the armed forces use technology to improve combat readiness. In a whirlwind two days, I visited all five branches of the military, and witnessed training for virtually every type of warfare. I saw how much our military personnel cherish speed—and the technology that delivers it. They believe that the United States is able to gather, analyze, distribute, and act on information faster than any other country on earth. Our military superiority, they told me, derives in large measure from our ability to unleash an information blitzkrieg—a lightning-fast data offensive that enables our forces to outsmart any potential enemy.

Over dinner, a Marine general and I discussed my belief that the information revolution depends on smart, creative people who understand how to take advantage of technology. The general agreed, citing the story of Air Force Captain Scott O'Grady, who was shot down while flying his F-16 fighter plane over enemy territory in Bosnia on June 2, 1995. His warning systems alerted him to an approaching surface-to-air missile. With only seconds to spare, Captain O'Grady sent a *Mayday* and ejected from the plane just as it was torn in half at an altitude of 8,000 feet. Landing safely in a forest, he tore off his parachute and threw it and himself into the underbrush, where he lay hidden, barely breathing, as enemy soldiers arrived to search the area. What seemed like endless minutes passed. Finally, the soldiers moved on.

For the next six days Captain O'Grady managed to stay one step ahead of the Serbs, surviving on leaves, insects, and rainwater he collected in his socks. Then, when he heard an aircraft flying low overhead, he whispered into his radio, "This is Basher 52–I'm alive." Within an hour, a U.S. helicopter carrying 20 Marines landed nearby, and O'Grady was whisked to safety as dozens of Serb soldiers moved in and surrounded the area.

If not for quick thinking, and swift responses enabled by state-of-the-art technology, Captain O'Grady wouldn't be alive. In his case, "speed is life" was literally true.

Speed saves lives in all fields, of course, but in business today it is the great differentiator, an essential survival tool. We live in a world where a company is measured by its ability to accelerate everything from manufacturing to marketing, from hiring to distributing. If we can produce or process something faster, we can often do it for less money, serve our customers better, and get a jump on our competitors. For almost any business these days, speed is indeed life.

Speed has always been my life. As founder and chief executive officer of the first truly global Internet media company, Lycos (now Terra Lycos), I was lucky enough to have been on the front lines of the Internet revolution—a revolution that was powered by technology but driven by speed.

In fact, the story of the Internet has been one that defies conventional business time lines. It took radio 38 years and television 13 years to build audiences of 50 million in the United States. The Internet attracted this critical mass in a mere three and a half years. And the Internet has hardly been operating in a vacuum. Its impact has been felt on virtually every company in the world; it has accelerated the way business is conducted in every industry.

In my nearly six years with Lycos, I saw the company move from concept to founding—for a while I was the first and only employee—through its initial public offering, acquisitions, and mergers, and finally through its own purchase by Terra Networks.

We launched the company in April 1995. Just nine months later, Lycos completed a public offering to become the fastest IPO (initial public offering) in NASDAQ history. Lycos evolved from a Web search engine—a gateway for users on their way to other destinations—into a hub, and from there, a comprehensive network of sites. We moved into Europe in 1996 via an alliance with the German media giant, Bertelsmann, and into Asia the next year. A series of acquisitions broadened our reach into homepage design and construction (Tripod), financial services (Quote.com), and online content (Wired Digital). We expanded into streaming media, music and videos, online shopping, investment information, and interactive entertainment. We broadened our role in Asia, Canada, and Latin America, and spun off our joint venture with Bertelsmann as Lycos Europe, a separate publicly traded business.

The Lycos Network has been described as the world's largest community. In any given month, nearly half of all Internet users—some 91 million people—visit Lycos to conduct searches, construct homepages, chat, look at news, check stocks, download files, or listen to the radio. Worldwide, its 61 million registered users view more than 350 million pages every day.

How did it all happen so quickly? The answer is that technology has taken us into a whole new dimension of time, what some call Internet time. It comes in three speeds: fast, faster, and instant, which means *right now*. With instant information and transactions, the Internet breaks all time barriers.

Brevity rules. On the Internet very little lasts, whether good or bad, and the wheel is being continually reinvented. Look at human communication. The Internet has quickly developed its own slang, symbols, and shorthand. Does anyone remember what writing a thank-you note with a fountain pen was like? Now imagine that same note sent as an instant message. Not only the form, but the content will be different. Less thoughtful? Perhaps. More direct and immediate? Absolutely.

In this rapid new world, almost instant innovation is essential. For CEOs and managers leading the charge, this can be trying stuff. Like her counterparts at other big companies, Hewlett-Packard CEO Carly Fiorina is probably more exhilarated than exhausted, but it's a close call. At a recent work force gathering, one H-P employee asked her, "What keeps you up at night?" Her answer: "Time. Because time, I believe, is not on any of our sides. In today's economy, faster is always better than slower, and sooner is always better than later. Always. Always. Always. That's tough discipline. It also happens to be necessary for survival. In this technology-driven world, the future is now. Seconds tick by and it is too late."

Fiorina is hardly the only chief executive feeling the burn. AOL's Steve Case put it this way in a recent speech: "You know the song, 'What a Difference a Day Makes?' Well, in our business, the song we sing is more like, 'What a Difference a Nanosecond Makes.' "

Is there a limit to all this acceleration? A point where the laws of nature will force things to slow down? Dick Sabot—who was the chairman of Tripod, a homepage-building service, when Lycos bought his company, and who now runs eZiba, a handicrafts e-tailer—doesn't think so. "When we joined Lycos, Internet time was dog years, seven for one human year. That's no longer true. We now speed through our goals at a pace that's double dog years. But a friend of mine thinks we're moving to fruit-fly years—50 generations in one year."

It's not surprising, then, that "speed is life" became a Lycos credo, one of its guiding principles, and a cornerstone of its success.

In 1995, many companies were striving to become search destinations on the Web. Magellan, Point, Open Text, Infoseek, and others clamored for market share. Then, in addition to ourselves, Excite, Yahoo!, and Infoseek completed successful IPOs within weeks of each other. We became known in the industry as the "Four Horsemen." While the four of us grew, the others, unable to capture funding or the public confidence it brings, simply faded away.

Venture capitalist Dan Nova saw business cycles compressed by years. "When I first started in venture capital," he told me not long ago, "you typically built a new business over a period of three to five years and took it public after five years of growth, development, and investment. But, suddenly, companies were going public almost overnight. In many cases, the old three-year cycle was reduced to a mere three months."

For managers, this new model changes everything. Years ago, Evelyn Wood devised "speed reading," a clever method that enabled managers to soak up long reports in what seemed like minutes. With a tip of the hat to Wood, I've written this chapter to be a "speed *leading*" course. It isn't intended for inveterate slowpokes who have no interest or idea what real speed is, except perhaps as a wake-up call. It's aimed at high-energy, or potential high-energy, employees and managers who appreciate speed and want to know how to exploit it for themselves and their organizations.

My "course" has six basic principles:

1. Be the first mover or very close to it

Amazon.com was the first mover in the e-tailing world of books, and has reaped enormous attention, and market share, as a result. Barnes & Noble was second and became a force by quickly adapting to the Internet demands of speed, ease, and reach. I'm not sure that it matters who was third because the game on that ballfield is over.

Success belongs to those who act first and pay close attention to detail. First movers beat the competition by setting a standard that anyone who follows has to not only match, but surpass.

In the early days, for instance, when Lycos was a search engine, the top contender in the browser market was Netscape. We attracted traffic to our site because we were accessible through a search button on Netscape's Web page. Many of our competitors had relationships with Netscape, but through hard work, perseverance, and a bit of luck, we won that coveted search button on their page. Suddenly, we leapt to the head of the pack.

A year later, we never would have nabbed that spot—too many companies were competing for it. We strengthened our brand by being first, which made Netscape want to renew our contract, and the process became cyclical. We were good because we were first, and we were first because we were good.

On December 30, 1997—the day before New Year's Eve—we were offered the chance to buy the Internet company Tripod. We only had a few minutes to decide and we immediately made an offer. If we hadn't acted quickly, Tripod would probably now be owned by America Online, and Terra Lycos wouldn't be the company it is today. I'll have more to say about the Tripod acquisition later in this book—my point here is that we were able to make the decision the moment it was presented to us.

Speed must be derived not from impulse or swagger but from being ever alert to opportunity and willing to seize it immediately. There is nothing haphazard about speed. A company must log many work hours, some slow and painstaking, in order to be ready to move instantly.

Caveat: We all know the warning "speed kills." It can and will—if not tempered by discipline, determination, and a balanced life. I obviously understand the need for speed in business, but it is also important to balance speed with thought, study, research, discussion, or just sitting still. Ironically, sometimes slowing down will get you where you want to go more quickly.

Paul Tagliabue, commissioner of the National Football League, makes a useful distinction between the need to plan slowly and carefully—and execute rapidly. He stepped me through the League's Internet strategy as an example: "If you anticipate the future right and plan for it strategically, you can move quickly, nimbly, and flexibly, but it doesn't have to be off the seat of your pants. Speed to execute something that has been thought out and planned for strategically can be very important. Our Internet network is an example. We spent about five years planning for it. We built a consensus in about six weeks, then we had to execute an entirely new concept in less than six months. But we succeeded. So speed was critical."

First-mover advantage is critical in every field, from art to science to politics. "Speed matters very much in the world of ideas," Richard Freeland, president of Northeastern University, told me: "Very often the scholar who produces an interesting new idea attracts publicity, comes to embody the idea, and gains tremendous advantages over his or her peers." In other words, even academia is a marketplace of ideas where first-movers win.

But if first-mover advantage is a universal truth, the Web gives it an entirely new business dimension. Companies can instantly spring a new product on a global scale, leaving competitors breathless. The catch is that those competitors are likely to respond much more quickly than in the past—and also globally. Like it or not, we do business in a world that is spinning ever faster.

2. Speed is all about adaptability

Charles Darwin said, "It is not the strongest of the species that survive, but that which best adapts to change."

The market is littered with one-trick ponies, companies that had great ideas but were unable to turn them into sustainable businesses. If Lycos had remained solely a search engine, it would have lost its audience years ago. There are countless examples of companies and even industries that didn't understand the sea change taking place around them, and, as a result, stood by watching helplessly as their sandcastles were swept away. It's really quite simple: Adapt or die.

Thirty plus years ago, believe it or not, the Justice Department considered IBM so powerful that it negotiated a consent decree restricting the company's market practices. It feared that IBM's strength was curbing competition. In fact, IBM was weak because it was inflexible, and it wound up curbing itself. In less than a generation, it missed three historic technology shifts.

The first occurred when IBM, fat and comfortable with its high-margin mainframe business, ignored the advent of the mini-computer, allowing upstarts such as Sun and Digital to take root. Next, IBM watched from the sidelines as the personal-computer revolution transformed corporate data processing, and the PC pioneers—Compaq, Dell, Intel, and Microsoft—seized the field. Finally, ever-myopic Big Blue saw the Internet solely as a tool to sell more computers, not as an engine for generating entirely new products and revenue.

With all its power and might, IBM could have easily been a dominant provider, but it let others capture a first-mover advantage—because it was slow to adapt to change. Fortunately the company eventually adapted. With the arrival of Lou Gerstner, the company that was common fodder for criticism, learned to move quickly again. Once awakened, this sleeping giant moved swiftly. Almost overnight, its revenues shifted from hardware to services and Gerstner completed one of the greatest corporate repositionings ever.

"Nothing has changed the fundamental economics of business," James E. Copeland, Jr., CEO of Deloitte Touche Tohmatsu, told *Chief Executive* magazine not long ago. "It's still good to have a lot of capital. It's still good to be big. The problem is when you let your bigness make you slow, or when you let your experience lead you to believe your way is the best way. Established companies that prosper are those that don't allow their success to lull them to sleep. They stay nimble in the marketplace."

As General Electric's legendary leader Jack Welch has often said: "If you're not fast and adaptable, you're vulnerable. This is true for every segment of every business in every country in the world."

Not only in business, but in every field from art to sport to war, speed requires adaptability. Just moving more quickly in the same direction is a prescription for obsolescence. But if your company is structured and primed to adapt rapidly, you can seize opportunity almost as quickly as you spot it. At really high speeds, you reach an edge that feels effortless, thoughtless, and paradoxically relaxing. This is the edge known to athletes and fighter pilots. It is when all your practice and hard work pays off and the actual *doing* just happens.

One of the benefits of speed is that it forces you to be open-minded, receptive to unconventional ideas and trial-and-error experiments. "When you're experimental," Dick Sabot told me, "you expect to succeed some of the time and fail on other occasions. There's a tolerance for making mistakes and building on them."

Adaptability makes the difference between complacency and conquest. Let's compare the way two media giants, Time Warner and Bertelsmann, responded to the Internet. Though both embraced it, one sought to adjust the Internet to its own practices, while the other willingly adapted.

Time Warner, run by some very talented people, was quick to respond to the Internet. It launched its Pathfinder Web site in 1995. Pathfinder was a compilation of Time Warner's many fine publications, including *Time, People*, and *Fortune* magazines—and was operational before most media companies had even begun to plan their sites. What Time Warner missed, however, was that the new medium demanded new content. What worked in a magazine didn't necessarily work on the Web. Time Warner believed that the overwhelming power of their brands, given enough time, would attract users. And they assumed that a company earning billions of dollars a year had plenty of time.

They were wrong. The people at Time Warner did not realize that the Web had spawned a personal revolution based on the power of individual choice. Through chats, message boards, and e-mail, users created a global village that let them research information, express their views, and connect with others who shared their interests and obsessions—all in the safety, comfort, and anonymity of their homes. Today, Pathfinder no longer exists.

Sites such as Tripod, on the other hand, provided the free software people needed to build their own Web sites. The reasons they built the sites was simple and primal—we all want attention, recognition, and a forum in which to share our accomplishments. Suddenly, there was a grassroots movement of cyberspace site builders, and vast networks of new Web users cropped up at an incredible rate.

What you had was a *personal* publishing revolution on a planetary scale, and Time Warner's old-model Pathfinder didn't address any of it. Tripod and its peers understood that the Web's added value was interactivity and empowerment. By contrast, Pathfinder was simply *Time* magazine on the Web, *People* on the Web, *Fortune* on the Web. The end result was that in 2000, Time Warner, with all its might, was acquired by AOL, one of the companies it believed it could crush.

At the other extreme was Bertelsmann, the 100-year-old German media giant. Bertelsmann, the most global of all media companies and parent of the publisher of this book, conducts business in 54 countries and is a leader in music, publishing, magazines, and television production. It, too, understood the significance of the Internet thanks to Thomas Middelhoff, its charismatic chairman and chief executive. I first met Thomas in 1997. We sat in his office in Germany and discussed the creation of a Lycos European joint venture. At that time, he was the executive in charge of Bertelsmann's multimedia business and had a reputation for extraordinary vision. Our conversation on that February day was all about the future. Using a hockey analogy, Thomas was never about where the puck has been, he was all about where the puck was going.

Rather than try to squelch the market shifts, Middelhoff has always welcomed them. He convinced his company to purchase 5 percent of AOL, accepted a seat on its board of directors, and, through a joint venture, ran AOL Europe. (The AOL-Time Warner combination resulted in the dissolution of the joint venture; in return, Bertelsmann will receive a payment of up to $8.25 billion.)

By means of these alliances Bertelsmann developed a worldwide audience for its products and content and has seen the return on its investment grow into billions.

Never resting, however, and showing his ability to embrace change, Middelhoff moved again. He boldly aligned its music division in support of Napster, the software that gave music away and that many feared was the industry's gravest danger. Once again, he looked change in the face, invited it in, and adapted accordingly. Darwin would be proud.

3. Fast and good is better than slow and perfect

Though I don't know if Bill Gates would agree, it strikes me that this principle is one of the cornerstones of the Microsoft empire. The first version of virtually every Microsoft winner, from Office to Windows, has gone to market in far less than perfect form. This timing is no accident: Microsoft uses first releases to draw customers who then help refine the product by finding the bugs that Microsoft doesn't want to slow down to address. Once customers pinpoint what's wrong, Microsoft promptly fixes it.

Some customers may feel a bit like guinea pigs, part of a grand Microsoft experiment in nudging the limits of customers' tolerance. The company's success, however, speaks for itself. EMC's Dick Egan agrees, pointing out that putting an imperfect product in a customer's hands is often the best and sometimes the only way to get needed feedback. "You can go out and do surveys and sometimes your audience will respond," he told me, "but if you actually have a product there in front of them, the attention and feedback you get is much better thought out and certainly more comprehensive." Kevin Kelley, the respected editor of *Wired* magazine, holds a similar point of view: "Wealth in the new regime flows directly from innovation, not optimization; that is, wealth is not gained by perfecting the known, but by imperfectly seizing the unknown."

The product that beats the competition is seldom the best, and it's never perfect. The longer you hold out for perfection, the less likely you are to achieve it, and you'll lose whatever competitive edge you may have—a lesson we learned the hard way at Lycos.

Yahoo! developed what is probably their strongest franchise with its financial-services products. After initially providing basic stock quotes, it evolved into one of the most comprehensive finance offerings on the Internet.

Long before Yahoo! launched its service, I envisioned a similar site. My mistake, however, was attempting to build a product so big and bold that I ended up building nothing. After conceiving the idea, we aligned with a division of Intuit operating out of Pittsburgh. Four months later, we were still perfecting our blueprint. Yahoo! in the meantime had launched a site and was gathering customers. Sure, we saw all the bugs in their release, but they had the first-mover advantage, and the market loved it. Every day, the concept became less novel.

We shifted potential partners many times during this search for perfection until finally, on a Friday, out of pure frustration, we set an up-and-running deadline of the following Monday. We just couldn't wait any longer. We met the deadline and eventually built a strong financial-services presence. Still, it was a sobering lesson. That we finally got our concept together in three days showed me that we could have completed it long before we did. We had a great idea and should have been satisfied with a good offering, instead we wasted time seeking the perfect one. As a result, we lost a sizeable piece of market share.

I should have listened to Warren Buffett, the fabled fount of old-economy wisdom, who once said, "I don't try to jump over seven-foot bars. I look around for one-foot bars that I can step over."

Don't misunderstand me: I'm not suggesting that it is ever acceptable to deliver shoddy products. Striving for quality should be a passion. Never stop thinking of ways to make your products better, but don't get stuck trying to achieve perfection. Release the product and, at the same time, continue to refine it.

It's important to balance the sometimes competing needs for speed and quality. Neither one can be allowed to dominate at the expense of the other. Work for a superb product at a break-neck pace until one objective begins to undercut the other—and then recalibrate. The goal is to maintain a healthy tension and keep the needs in tandem, while making sure that you're growing in ways that give you an edge over the competition.

In an imperfect world, the quest for perfection often leads to blind alleys, frustration, and failure. Be content with being first and sweeten your victories with pride in your product as you continue to improve it. As Ford Motor crowed: "Quality is job one." Great slogan and great ideal—as long as you don't confuse quality with perfection.

In certain industries, of course, perfection is mandatory, especially when safety is at stake. We need look no further than the Firestone crisis to appreciate the human and business costs associated with poor products. When weighing the issue of quality versus speed, I find that answering a few basic questions helps me strike the right balance and make the right decision:

- What are the costs of delay?
- What are the costs of a less-than-perfect product?
- From my customers' perspective, do I hurt or strengthen the company with a rollout today?
- How quickly can my competitors respond?

4. Follow your gut

"I sometimes feel like I'm behind the wheel of a race car," America Online's CEO Steve Case noted during a recent speech. "I need to keep my eyes on the horizon, but I also need to keep my attention on the rear-view mirror to see who's gaining on me.

From the passenger seat, consumers are telling me where they want to be dropped off and when, and behind me my shareholders and business partners are engaged in loud back-seat driving. One of the biggest challenges is that there are no road signs to help navigate. And, in fact, every once in a while, a close call reminds me that no one has even yet determined which side of the road we're supposed to be driving on. And the finish line is a long, long way away."

I think anyone who has worked in today's economy can relate all too well to that comment. In these unnerving times, top managers can't afford much introspection and had best convince their most important audience—themselves—that they know what they're doing. If they don't know, who does? As Hewlett-Packard's plainspoken Fiorina says: "Know yourself, trust your whole self, and don't blink."

While I'd like to say that all our moves at Lycos were models of deliberation, fit for business textbooks, the truth is messier and much more interesting. At times, events moved so fast that we had to rely on our gut instincts and precious little else. We often brought out new products for one reason—because we could—and for the most part, this approach worked.

Lycos' IPO came about in a similar way. I had no experience with investment banking or public offerings, and so, as with so much else at that time, I found myself in the middle of a crash course. In late 1995, I received a call from a research analyst who had been part of a team courting the company. He told me he was about to begin working with a competitor of ours but wanted to give us one final opportunity to move forward with his firm. Would we be interested?

I spent much of the night on the phone talking to our directors. The timing was well ahead of anything we had envisioned, but it was a striking opportunity. My instincts told me to seize it, and our initial public offering was completed 100 days later.

Relying on your gut is usually a pretty effective way to

hire people, as well. When interviewing a candidate, I often knew within the first five minutes whether or not I was interested. I found myself either coaxing the person to come to join us, or looking at my watch to figure out how quickly I could end the interview. I wasn't looking for perfection, I was looking for chemistry—a certain indefinable connection that told me this person and I could work together.

Ted Philip, our chief financial officer, is an example of one such hire and among the best decisions I've ever made. When I first met him, it only took me a few minutes, literally, to realize that he was a winner and I wanted him on the Lycos team. As we spoke, his obvious leadership skills, wisdom, and presence only increased my excitement—and I pursued him aggressively. At that time, Ted was happy in his position at Disney, and it took about a month to persuade him to leave. Ted was a spectacular fit. Some thought that his low-key style made us temperamental opposites, but as a black belt at Tae Kwon Do, one who races jet skis at 80 miles an hour, snowmobiles at 120, and motorcycles at full throttle, and with a passion for leadership, his is a life that operates very much in the fast lane.

5. Speed is a cultural value

When Lycos started out, we not only lacked a long-range business plan, but we saw no reason to have one. We assumed that given the nature of the Internet, any plan would be obsolete in three months. Instead, we chose to be flexible, intuitive, and pragmatic. We scrambled for market share anywhere we thought we could find it. While hungrily seeking revenue, we focused on trying to differentiate ourselves in the market.

Much of our challenge lay in figuring out what would work. We wanted to take everyday items and experiences and put them online: yellow pages, dating services, weather updates, and road maps. Whenever I read a press release touting a competitor's new product or service, I thought, "Damn, we can do that." Being fast and first was vital because, in addition to new customers, it provided exceptional media coverage.

We worked to build a culture in which getting things done quickly was the organizing principle. In his book, *Business at the Speed of Thought*, Bill Gates wrote: "Speed of business has been limited by moving information around, but with digital tools moving that information at the speed of light, the only constraint is how well you use your knowledge workers, your thinkers, to re-act to what is going on, to plan new products to make sure you are using all of your resources in the right way." Technology gives us abundant information. Putting it to work effectively is the job of people. Creating a culture that encourages lightning-fast imple-mentation is the duty of the company's leaders.

Jan Horsfall, now president and CEO of Phonefree.com, was marketing vice president at Lycos during this turbulent time. In a recent conversation with me, he remembered those early day like this:

> The real win for Lycos was speed. Web users wanted easy access to information, but Yahoo! had already carved out that feature. So we focused instead on the fact that users also wanted things faster. We ended up making the site quicker to use by cutting out size. We did a ton of us-ability studies: speed involved not only site performance but also how fast people could find things. It forced us to get into the navigational structure of the site to under-stand how people moved around. We did very intensive user studies just to figure out how people clicked from place to place.
>
> All this forced the company to really focus on what the consumer felt was important. We brought numerous engi-neers to Waltham, who feverishly looked for ways to make the Lycos site go faster, whether it was the way we were hosted, whether it was the size of the pages. Before long, the entire company was wrapped around this idea of speed.

So many business maxims—"Cut your losses" or "Damn the torpedoes, full speed ahead"—are based on the need to move relentlessly forward as fast as possible. Speed is of the essence, and needs to be ingrained throughout the organization. With products, marketing, distribution, even people, you need to act swiftly. If you're a pro football coach, for instance, trying to build a winning team in a few preseason weeks, you can't afford to gently nurture someone's nascent talent. You build on the strong players and cut the weak.

I made a mistake with our first marketing executive. It was clear we were never going to be on the same wavelength. Four months after I hired him, I fired him. Firing employees isn't something to be proud of, but all too often I see organizations delaying the inevitable, creating a "death by a thousand cuts" scenario that leaves both the employee and the company harmed.

Do what works as fast as you can, and don't waste time worrying about how closely your methods fit the models in business textbooks, because these days those textbooks are out of date almost as soon as they're printed.

6. Avoid analysis paralysis

Looking back on his seemingly flawless record at General Electric, even the mighty Jack Welch once acknowledged, "My biggest mistake was agonizing too long over difficult decisions. I should have done it faster."

Nothing is more exasperating than what I call analysis paralysis or freeze-ups. You're facing a big challenge and suddenly your mind goes blank, your tongue thickens, your limbs slacken. Freeze-ups can happen to anyone—an actor forgets lines, a salesperson blocks the top customer's name, a new chief executive botches a speech to skeptical stockholders. They can affect star athletes: A superb shortstop like the Yankees' Chuck Knobloch can't throw to first base; Tiger Woods begins slicing into sand traps on the fifteenth hole; U.S. Open defending champion Serena Williams is unable to avoid serving one double-fault after another.

Why do people freeze-up? Often, it's because they start analyzing what they're doing instead of just doing it. Even if you achieve the aerobatic grace of, say, a fighter pilot maneuvering at supersonic speeds, your spell can be broken. Fear intrudes; you become self-conscious. Focus vanishes; you panic and are paralyzed. Your moment passes and you fail.

Speed is the secret weapon, the weapon without which battles are lost, fortunes squandered, and breakthroughs undiscovered. Speed is liberating because those with quick minds and quick steps accept no limits.

As Ralph Waldo Emerson put it: "In skating over thin ice our safety is in our speed." Life is too fleeting to waste precious moments avoiding, dithering, fearing, hesitating, or regretting. To act is to live. To act fast is to live fully.

You let up, you lose

3

NOT LONG AGO, I had occasion to gain a new perspective on a subject I thought I knew very well—the art of winning.

Former President Clinton and I were both guests at a small dinner party in Cambridge, Massachusetts, and he was discussing the advice he gave to his wife, Hillary, when she decided to run for the U.S. Senate. First, he told her, she must be prepared to lose.

I was surprised to hear him say that. In my experience, winners become winners largely because they never consider losing. They never stop going the extra mile, the extra yard, the extra inch.

President Clinton, however, had a broader view. Emphasizing that you can never guarantee an outcome, you have to recognize that failure is a possibility, and be prepared for it, as well as for winning. His logic struck me as particularly perceptive because it reflects a view I had not seriously considered—a solid foundation for success must always include a detailed analysis of failure. Through such an analysis you can chart a course that underscores what's working against you, and build a plan to sidestep or overcome it.

Downside management was the subject of the President's second bit of wisdom. He told Hillary she was obligated to do *everything* in her power to win. He thought that she could live with her possible defeat if, and only if, she had successfully communicated her message to every New York voter. If each voter who opposed her could say, "I have an in-depth understanding of what you represent, and I don't like it," then, she had done her job. But, if she lost because she failed to make her message crystal clear, or, worse yet, didn't give some people the opportunity to hear her message, she would be losing because she hadn't worked hard enough. Defeat for that reason would be hard to live with.

With different words, the President was supporting a philosophy about which I am passionate. Simply put, "You let up, you lose," and, you lose for an unacceptable reason—you didn't work hard enough.

< D O W N S I D E   M A N A G E M E N T >

I was first introduced to the concept of downside management by Dan Nova, the venture capitalist who also introduced me to Lycos. He is a devout practitioner and applies it to all aspects of his professional life. That it does not involve a complex methodology should not trick you into underestimating its efficacy. The first step in downside management is to identify all possible negative outcomes that could result from a given set of circumstances. The next step is to develop plans and workarounds that may mitigate them. Having identified the worst-case outcomes and devised methods for approaching them, you are equipped to make risk-balanced decisions.

Downside management can be used in infinite sets of circumstances. For instance, let's apply it to what many psychological surveys rate as one of the top three sources of stress in this country—a job change. The negative repercussions are, in this case, easy to create: You change jobs and end up either fired from or hating your new workplace. Had you applied downside management, you would have anticipated a myriad of issues, including: How will this new job prepare me for the one that follows it? Am

I in a financial situation to leave abruptly if, for some reason, I have to? If it does not work out, will my reputation be harmed? After you answer all of these questions, and many more like them, you can make a far more informed decision and feel confident, it is the right one. Downside management prepares you to face and manage any consequence that was at all foreseeable.

< T H E   S I E G E   O F   N E T S C A P E >

The President's advice provoked me to think about Lycos' formative days. I thought, too, about lessons I learned early on that ultimately saved the company from possible disaster. In early 1996, Lycos' business model, as well as those of our key competitors, was fairly fluid, and, to some extent, our audiences were based on a camaraderie among the handful of companies devoted solely to the Web at that time. The advertising models that we're familiar with today were then in embryonic stages, at most. Often, users discovered a site because they were led there by a series of reciprocal links from one Web site to another. In other words, we shuffled users back and forth among noncompeting sites. The idea was to enable each individual audience to grow more rapidly. Lycos, for example, encouraged users to explore Geocities and, in return, Geocities posted a small graphic inviting its users to search the Web with Lycos. Geocities is now owned by Yahoo! and, needless to say, those links are long gone. But at one point, as much as 20 percent of Geocities' audience arrived there by following our link. The most notable of these linking relationships we had was with Netscape.

As one of the Internet's only viable browsers, Netscape was in an enviable position. It was the Web's "town center" or hub, and perhaps its first. It worked like this: if you were an Internet user, you used a Netscape browser, which meant that you traveled through its pages and computers at some point during your online journey. To say that a site's existence was determined by whether or not it had exposure on Netscape is not hyperbole. We were lucky; Netscape provided a very prominent link to Lycos that appeared each time a user clicked on the "search" area. In fact, that link remains a key feature of browser technology today. And, the price was right—it was free.

But, beginning in March 1996, our simple unstructured arrangement began to unravel. Literally days before our IPO was to take place, Netscape informed us that, starting immediately, it would be charging us $5 million annually for the link. We were dumfounded.

At that point, Lycos' total revenue for its entire lifetime was less than $1 million. Netscape's timing could not have been worse for us. We had just completed two weeks on a road show describing our company and, of course, its financial model to prospective institutional investors, and certainly this expense had not been included.

Near the end of our IPO road show, we decided to sign the contract with Netscape. We were, in fact, at the "call down," stage which is a lengthy meeting or conference call with lawyers, accountants, and investment bankers at which the business provides a representation stating that no material changes had occurred between that present day and the completion of their exhaustive due diligence, which was, in our case, about three weeks earlier.

Despite the obvious problems, moving forward with the Netscape contract was an easy decision. We had no choice. Over 50 percent of our traffic came from its single search button. That I dreaded having to announce the incremental $5 million at the calldown is an understatement. With a horrible sense of defeat, we pictured our tightly scripted IPO collapsing in flames.

We decided to delay the offering by a few days, which left us fewer than 48 hours to develop a plan. First, we worked through downside management alternatives. We prepared a new financial model and arranged for the analysts working for our investment banks to brief Wall Street on the change. We developed a workable plan. The result was spectacular—we raised over $40 million (a large sum by any measure, but particularly for an Internet offering in 1996) and watched the price of Lycos rise over 40 percent in its first day of trading.

One year later, Netscape hit us with the second stage of the same missile. When our contract came up for renewal, the team at Netscape told us that they were no longer including Lycos on their page. They had a long list of companies who wanted that access, and our brand, according to them, wasn't strong enough, our service wasn't good enough, or our relationships solid enough to meet their standards.

It was obvious that this was not a bargaining ploy; it was a final ruling allowing no appeal. The Netscape executives wouldn't even take our calls. Whether or not they were treating a small, struggling company unfairly was beside the point. Foreshadowing Bill Clinton's advice, we had to recognize that we hadn't worked hard enough. If Netscape was eliminating Lycos for the wrong reasons, the root cause was still us: We hadn't given them enough reason to choose us. It was our job to show Netscape exactly why we were the right search partner to feature on its site.

Our vice president of business development, Ben Bassi, and I flew out to Mountain View, California. We virtually lived at Netscape for the next month, and were determined not to leave until we had our day in court. With pagers, cell phones, and laptops, we sat in and around the company's buildings until we became fixtures that were impossible to ignore.

We tried every tactic we could imagine to breach Netscape's resistance. We made call after call to the manager in charge of the Internet-search program, and her boss, Mike Homer, the company's marketing vice president. That Netscape was immersed in battles with Microsoft and AOL did nothing to help us win their attention. Had we let up, we surely would have lost the Netscape position and probably the company as well. Finally, we were able to leverage a contact with a member of Netscape's board. Through that person, we got our day in court.

We convinced the Netscape team that our participation was vital to their program's success. We tried to express our momentum and our determination to become a powerful force. We were resolved to succeed and, if we did, it would be bad business to ignore us.

We aggressively used the fact that Microsoft was including us on its page—did Netscape want to be left out? When online viewers looked for a page to find Lycos, as thousands more did every day, did Netscape actually want them to have to go to Microsoft's page?

Though each tactic played a role in getting us reinstated on the Netscape browser, I believe our determination and relentless passion were most important. Had we let up, we certainly would have lost, and we weren't willing to let that happen. We presented ourselves as a desirable business partner with a brand that was substantially stronger than they were acknowledging. We conveyed our conviction that Lycos was not then the company it would become in 12 months. "If you don't include us here," we said, "you're going to wake up and wish you had." In the end, they believed us.

Our perseverance was the decisive factor. On that subject, Richard Freeland, president of my alma mater, Northeastern University, observes that, "In the world I have lived in, speed counts and swiftness counts. But, in the end, the race is to those who persevere in pursuit of a strong vision, not just those who are fastest out of the block." Ted Philip, Lycos' chief financial officer, believes that, "Most people have the intelligence to do a pretty good job, but real success is a matter of which person is going to outwork the others.... It's all about perseverance."

The Netscape experience was a harrowing ordeal from which I learned a lot.

1. Follow the concept of "You let up, you lose" every day—steady execution should always be the rule. Our mistake was in waiting until the 11th hour to enact our plan. For example, we should have realized earlier that we had a

board relationship. Often, you can avoid the need for crisis management altogether with good, methodical execution at every step throughout the process.

2. If I learned anything from my transactions with Netscape, I learned that in order to successfully execute any business strategy, you must be willing to make the most of every possible advantage. If this sounds familiar, it is a restatement of President Clinton's advice to Mrs. Clinton regarding her eventually successful Senate race—she was obligated to do everything in her power to win.

3. A smart businessperson learns to recognize when she is continuing an already lost or futile battle, on the one hand, and surrendering too early, on the other. Both can be destructive, and knowing the difference can be crucial. The balance can be difficult to discern; against all odds, momentum swings and shifts the dynamics of a competitive landscape. Victory comes to those who demand it.

<THE ROAD TO THE T-SHIRT>

Describing what it takes to win, Vince Lombardi said: "There's only one way to succeed in anything, and that is to give it everything. I do, and I demand that my players do.... If you aren't fired with enthusiasm, you'll be fired with enthusiasm."

Lycos' unrelenting passion to win is a crucial part of its foundation. In fact, the words "You let up, you lose" were printed on a framed, faded T-shirt that hung outside my office. I discovered the T-shirt when the company was preparing for our initial public offering.

We were engaged in the grueling, demanding, and challenging business of writing the prospectus. It was particularly difficult because we were outlining long-term plans and strategies for the corporation when we didn't fully understand them ourselves. With corporate officers, investment bankers, lawyers, and accountants representing all parties involved with the offering, we were also drafting the road-show presentation for investors. This entailed an exhaustively detailed description of the financial model and corporate strategy. We argued endlessly over the precise wording of this 70- to 80-page document. At the end of one of these long days, our group ventured out for a beer. In the bar, I spotted a man who had to weigh 400 pounds playing pool; he was wearing the T-shirt.

We all loved the message and Dan Nova wagered $20 that I could not get the shirt. I spent 45 minutes trying to quite literally talk the shirt off his back. Finally my persistence won the day; I paid him a few dollars, collected my $20 from Dan, and had my prized possession. The shirt was framed and hung outside my office ever since. And, it wasn't there for the benefit of employees and visitors—it was there for me. It was the first thing I saw each morning, and reminded me that if you let up in the battle, you lose your discipline, determination, and, of course, the victory.

<SUCCESS STARTS WITH COMMITMENT>

I was in high school when I first realized the importance of commitment. A mediocre student with especially poor grades in Latin, I studied by cramming the night before the tests. But for one particular Latin exam, I prepared for days in advance. I got a good grade, but far more pertinent was the lesson in life I learned: You will have much more control over your destiny if you are determined and committed to work hard for what you want.

My career has afforded me the opportunity and pleasure of meeting and getting to know many accomplished people. Significantly, all those I admire share a commitment to hard work. Indeed, and this is important, although they will use different words, each has his or her own version of "You let up, you lose." That is, each has a perspective on the relationships among success, commitment, perseverance, and hard work. If the views share an essential core, which they do, they remain, at the same time, unique. In this section, I want to share a few such perspectives.

ABC news correspondent Sam Donaldson and I met recently to talk about his fledgling Internet broadcast. Committed to hard work, Donaldson believes that the Web will be a powerful news force and he wants to be sure he is in front of it. In fact, he has credited this commitment to accomplishing his goals for his present-day success. After "I got in the news business, I devoted myself single-handedly, single-mindedly to it," Donaldson said. "I mean, I lived, and breathed, and ate it. I worked 24 hours a day." Donaldson says about success: "You have to work harder than the next person. You have to take dirty jobs. You have to take less money than you can live on, or certainly than you want, and certainly than you think you are worth. You have to work on weekends, you have to work nights, you have to get up at 2:00 in the morning. You have to skip your birthday, your anniversary, the kid's birthday." In other words, you put your life on hold such that little else matters. That is perserverance.

Donald R. Keough, chairman of Allen & Company, and former president of The Coca-Cola Company, has a further perspective on determination. He told me: "There are periods when good things happen, and suddenly you hit a plateau." Don pays attention to how people react to plateaus. "A lot of people just stop. They tell themselves they aren't getting any breaks, the market's against them, competition is killing them—the whole litany of rationalizations. But a plateau is exactly when they should grade their own performance and get themselves ready for the next opportunity. It's exactly in those limbo periods that perseverance is most essential." In a world that counts in nanoseconds, the difference between winners and losers is often based on whose commitment to succeed is stronger.

Charles Conn, CEO of Ticketmaster Online City Search, one of our proposed merger partners in the USA transaction, believes that "perseverance accounts for 75 to 80 percent of winning." He told me: "People place enormous value on incisive, strategic, or analytical thinking. Certainly when I was a partner at McKinsey & Company, I would have examined the strategic thinking, and people's intellect and success before getting involved in any company. Now, five years later, my priorities have changed. Good ideas and sound strategic thinking are important, but being fast on your feet so that you're ready to respond to change is even more critical. We live in a world where change is so rapid that strategic plans need to be rewritten quarterly, if not monthly. I think persistence is a good word. Stick to the vision of what you want to create."

Paul Cellucci, the governor of Massachusetts, told me that in his business—state government—"perseverance is everything." He explained, "I'm from a small town in the central part of the state, a Republican in a Democratic state, and I worked my way up, starting in local government. I was elected to the state legislature as a House member, where I served for eight years before being elected to the state senate, where I served for six. I was elected lieutenant governor with Bill Weld in 1991, and became the governor when he left to seek the U.S. ambassadorship in Mexico. Then I won the election in 1998 in my own right. You have to have a lot of determination and perseverance to get from where I started to where I am."

Cellucci remembers one time in particular when it would have been easy to give up: "I think back to when I ran for the state legislature the first time in 1976. It was two years after Watergate, which was not exactly a great time to be running as a Republican. It was not a good year and I knew I would have to work hard. I remember on July 5, I started ringing doorbells and planned to ring every bell in the district. After four hours on that first day, I wondered if I ought to have my head examined. But I rang every bell—7,000 doors. And when the votes were counted on election day I won by 1,000 votes. Some people call it perseverance—a lot of times in the political world we say you have to have fire in your belly. You have to be determined and you have to persevere."

Echoing Governor Cellucci's opinion is Desh Deshpande, chairman of Sycamore Networks. Desh is a serial entrepreneur and is building one of the Northeast's cornerstone technology companies. He laid it out for me this way: "This is my third startup and when you begin these things, they are Herculean tasks. If you really look at it, you have no chance of winning against all the guys who have lots of resources, people, money, and talent. The only reason why yours can be successful is because you believe you're going to win. Winning doesn't come easy. It comes with lots of problems and lots of hurdles. Something can go wrong every day. I think you really have to be a born optimist to survive in this business."

When I asked Desh if he could recall a time when most, if not all, of the company's executives wanted to change directions or even give up altogether, but his persistence carried the day, he said, "It happens every day, even now, because of the type of company we're trying to build. The type of company that I've always attempted to build is big game. That means you have to push hard, which can be painful. If you're competing in a tight market space, you don't win by miles, you win by inches, because everybody in the market is very smart and competitive. You have to push very hard and when you do, you tend to fail, at least in little things. Hopefully you'll win the overall game."

Still, Deshpande says, when things get difficult, people "raise doubts about whether you're doing the right thing, whether you can actually get there. I don't see that as a one-time problem. You have that problem when you run a company with 1 person, 10 people, 100, or 1,000 people." The challenge for a leader is to keep yourself and a team focused and motivated through each stage of a company's development. To really capture its power, a "You let up, you lose" mindset is required in all environments, 365 days a year.

When I first met Naveen Jain, InfoSpace's founder, chairman, and CEO, he was a product manager at Microsoft locked in a daily battle with corporate bureaucracy. But, as with so many entrepreneurs, he became restless until one day he gathered the determination to put all at risk and start his own business. Naveen summed up his attitude quite well, "You have to believe in something in life. In some sense, believing in something and executing it are not enough because, after a while, a lot more people have vision than succeed in life. To be successful in life, there are a few qualities that a person has to have in addition to a good idea and the capacity to execute it. More than anything else, you have to have a passion for success. That means you have to believe that you can succeed no matter what gets in your way. That's where the perseverance comes in. That means, once you believe you are on the right track, you have to continue to persevere. In some sense, I think that we did that at Info-Space. We had a great idea—that wireless was going to be very, very big, way back in 1996 when nobody was looking at it. And we continued to persevere and build the right technology and, today, we are enjoying the benefits of that."

It's amazing how many perceived "overnight successes" reached their pinnacle through years of dogged determination. We always hear about the crowning achievements of our leaders. What we seldom hear about is the never-ending creativity, persistence, and good old-fashioned hard work that made those achievements possible. Recently, Robert Kraft, owner of the New England Patriots, told me his story of perseverance in the face of adversity. "I love football, I love the Patriots, so I tried to figure out a way that I could get an edge to buy the team. In 1985 or 1986, I paid a lot of money for a ten-year option to control the parking around the stadium. That was my first edge. Then in 1988 when the then current stadium owners, the Sullivan family, declared bankruptcy, a lot of people tried to buy the team, but we always controlled the land. I bought the stadium out of bankruptcy by outbidding the then-owner of the team, Victor Kiam. So then I owned the land, the stadium, and controlled the revenue streams from the team. Every time someone tried to buy the team, that person had to talk to me about the land, the stadium, and how to get out of the lease.

"About 18 or 20 suitors came to buy the team. I just kept my head down and kept running the stadium as well as I could. Finally, I got a chance to bid on the team and actually buy it in 1994. It took almost ten years of hard work and persevering through many setbacks. But, it eventually happened. With the exception of meeting my wife 37 years ago, everything good that has happened in my life has been through hard work, perseverance, and overcoming adversity."

Tom Stemberg, founder and chief executive officer of Staples, told me another such story. "A professor once said that the large number of people who achieve a reasonable modicum of success reveals that a lot of people were born with talent, but the ones who really succeed are those who work their butts off to get somewhere. I think that perseverance has been a huge factor in my career. Nothing comes easy. The first Staples store wasn't a success. It took a while for people to figure out what we were all about. Had you bet after the first week or month that this would become a $10-billion business one day, not many people would have bet with you. The majority of the $8,000 we did our first day was from friends and relatives. We actually paid people $10 in advance to shop in the store, and they promised to do it. Of the 20 people we paid, none showed up, which speaks to how hard it was going to be to get people to try something new."

Tom used his international expansion as yet another example of keeping your head down and sticking with something until you get it right. "The eight years and at least three major transformations it has taken us to create a profitable business in Europe is an example of our perseverance. We started out with joint ventures which didn't work, so we sent a U.S. management team to run these businesses that had been run by locals. We realized we needed to centralize, which we tried to do in England, but we found that we couldn't get people from the continent to move to England. So, then we reconfigured it again, moved the headquarters to Brussels, finally got the Europeans to run it, and now we're creating success. But that was an awfully long time, a lot of steps, and a lot of losses along the way."

It should not be surprising that over the ages we continue to hear a similar message from those who have succeeded. Timothy Forbes, who is *Forbes* magazine's chief operating officer told me about the trials and tribulations his company faced nearly a hundred years ago. "It's one thing to have a great idea; it's quite another to build a business around an idea. That's the tough part. My grandfather founded this company in 1917, and for the first dozen years it was tremendously successful. In 1928, Hearst offered to buy the magazine for a million dollars, a lot of money for a Scottish immigrant. He turned it down. Later, he must have kicked himself. The Depression almost killed the magazine. Between 1930 and the late 1950s, it struggled. My grandfather was also a columnist for Hearst newspapers. His columnist's income kept the magazine afloat. That and what he called Scotch week, which meant that one week every month you worked for free. You still had a job, but effectively you took a 25 percent pay cut. Obviously, the eventual happy outcome derived from grandfather's terrific persistence—and all of us are very, very grateful."

<WINNING IS CONTAGIOUS>

I have always been inspired by Vince Lombardi's speech, "What it Takes to Be Number 1." As a student, a salesman, and a CEO, I felt uplifted daily when I read the copy that has hung on my walls for years. Its focus is "Attitude," a basic ingredient in winning. In Lombardi's words, "You've got to be smart to be number one in any business. But, more importantly, you've got to play with your heart, with every fiber of your body. If you're lucky enough to find a guy with a lot of head and a lot of heart, he's never going to come off the field second. Running a football team is no different than running any other kind of organization—an army, a political party or a business. The principles are the same. The object is to win—to beat the other guy."

At Lycos, we were interested in winning, not just for the next paycheck or even the next big event, but for its own sake. The experience of joining others in a common fight for collective victory is exhilarating. We have experienced it many times at Lycos, but none more exquisitely than when we finalized the deal to sell the company. A winning spirit is powerful. "Confidence is contagious and so is lack of confidence" is Lombardi's straightforward description of how teams function. A team will be motivated to perform excellently if it has confidence in itself and is led by committed managers.

Ted Philip, our chief financial officer and chief operating officer, was born with the Lycos ethos. As I mentioned in the previous chapter, I was lucky enough to hire him when he was a finance vice president at The Walt Disney Company, where he arranged financing for virtually every Disney film over the previous five years; in addition, the concept of the 100-year bond on Wall Street is his. He instilled his passion for his work in his team, whose pride inspired the entire company, and spurred a self-reinforcing cycle. Eventually, Ted's team's ethos became the norm. Examples of this group's determination abound. Tom Guilfoile, senior vice president of finance and administration, perhaps the hardest working person in the company, is one. The ultimate team player, he was famous for working around the clock for three and four days straight anytime a job needed to get done.

One time when we had run out of office space, Tom moved himself out of his office into what we called the computer room, which was really a closet, five feet by three feet, where we had the phone system and the computers, as well as a couple of small servers. His first problem was that these machines kicked off massive amounts of heat, keeping the room at a consistent 90 degrees-plus. The bigger problem came when he was working late one night and discovered that the door had been locked from the outside. He was stuck in that sweltering closet for about eight hours. But as morning came it was clear that he had not missed a beat as he continued to work throughout the night. We used to tease him because he endured six months straight of a three-hour daily drive without heat or air conditioning in his car—he was working such long hours that he didn't have time to get it fixed.

That was pretty typical of our people; all had a passionate work ethic. On several occasions, employees slept on my office couch because they worked so late that they decided not to drive home. I believe that people chose to put in that kind of time because, as team members, they knew they were contributing something, and certainly, they were appreciated. We created a particular culture with a healthy sense of camaraderie, and it spread throughout the organization.

While people are driven to win for the pure gratification of winning, that doesn't mean that stock options and employee ownership aren't key contributors as well. Each employee was granted stock options at some level in the company, with over 200 individuals accumulating more than $1 million in value. If you own a piece of the company, it is only logical that you feel more concerned about it. When Lycos was about a year old, Brian Lucy, our controller, discovered that the cleaning people had accidentally thrown away the extra copies of our first annual report. Brian climbed into the dumpster, dug through its contents, found the reports, and brought them back to the office. While he was in there, he found some broken furniture, which he reassembled and used for the next few months to furnish our expanding offices.

Good leaders guide by example. I could cite dozens of successful CEOs who do so, but Mel Karmizan, CEO of CBS until its acquisition, and now president and chief operating officer of Viacom, is an excellent example. Mel embodies the spirit of "You let up, you lose." With exacting standards, he seems to be reviewing his employees' performances every day. It is accepted within the culture; people expect and live by it. Not long ago, Mel sent me a video e-mail pitching some CBS services. He ended with the words, "You will hear from our salesperson in the next few days—if you don't, let me know, and you will hear from his replacement." Not surprisingly, the network has excelled under his regime.

Along with determination, perseverance, and commitment, the capacity for passion is a critical ingredient of success. As Ernie Allen, head of the National Center for Missing & Exploited Children, told me: "The really successful people in life and . . . in this society, invariably, have passion with a vision for where they want to go, and are not going to let the impediments that all encounter detract them. They're going to get there." The most successful people "bring that sort of commitment to whatever they do."

< FOCUS IS FOREVER >

I want to close this chapter with a tribute to two individuals who will never lose their focus. One is the film director Ron Howard, and the other is the physician Judah Folkman, known for his breakthrough cancer research. Each is an exceptional leader whose level of success is one that few of us even aspire to. Since I have devoted this chapter to describing what, in my view, makes a winner, I want to close with brief descriptions of two men that are extraordinary, even among winners.

I first met Ron Howard when he was considering launching an Internet site that would enhance independent film production. We spent a good deal of time strategizing how Lycos might play a role in the new venture. Committed to producing only the highest quality entertainment for his audiences, Howard, while genuine and unassuming, is an extremely intense and focused man. As Ron described it to me, each new film is an adventure that requires total commitment from him and everyone—actor, grip, and cameraman—on the set. Recently, Ron was inducted into the American Academy of Achievement and in his own words described his determination. "If I can give myself credit for anything, it's probably not taking [my success] for granted. I don't think I've ever assumed it was going to go on forever unless I kept earning my way, earning my keep.... I never want to coast on past performances. It's probably one of the reasons I wanted to become a director, because I wanted to be able to control those opportunities [and] ... keep doing good work."

Dr. Judah Folkman is involved in work that is surely more important than either mine or Ron Howard's. I met Dr. Folkman not long ago at Children's Hospital in Boston where, along with the Dana Farber Cancer Center, also in Boston, he spends most of his professional time. Leading a team of extremely focused researchers in trying to unravel the science of cancer, Dr. Folkman cannot measure his results every quarter, and rarely can he claim victory at the end of a year, though he has had more than a few successes. Instead, he delivers results over a lifetime, with each one requiring thousands of small steps along the way. Dr. Folkman explains his determination in the face of adversity this way:

There's a fine line between persistence and obstinacy, and you never know when you've crossed it.... As I observed other scientists and read about them, [I noted that] many ... had given up. Fleming gave up on penicillin. He discovered it in the late '20s, tried to purify it, failed, and wrote in 1932, "I give up ... This will never be useful because it's too unstable." And so, it waited until 1941 till Florey and Chaine could figure out how to purify it. All three got the Nobel prize. So, had [Fleming] persisted, he might have had it many years earlier.

The obstacles [for me] mainly were in the very beginning, in the late '60s, when we proposed the idea that tumors need to recruit their own private blood supply. That was met with almost universal hostility, and ridicule, and disbelief by other scientists, because [it contradicted] the dogma at that time. Then, after we showed it was important, which took us about five years . . . everyone said—pathologists, surgeons, basic scientists—said, "You're studying dirt. There will be no such molecules." And then when we actually proved that there was—that was now 1983 (starting in the late '60s), we had the first molecule. . . . They said, "Well, but you'll never prove that that's what tumors use."

The nay-sayers keep coming . . . say[ing], "Well, it works in mice, but it won't work in people." So I say, "So what? Should we not test? Should I stop because you know for sure?"

I say, "Will you sign?" I have a little book that I carry, I say, "Will you sign for me? Because you're so sure [this won't work in people], I can just publish your remarks directly and save a lot of government and taxpayers' money, and we won't do the experiments. We won't test in humans. We'll just say it won't work."

In science, the arts, business, and most, if not all, other fields, success is earned the same way: relentless determination. A cynic might say they were lucky. I think not. My father used to tell me that luck is when preparation meets opportunity, and hence you make your own luck. All of the people I have discussed in this chapter reflect Calvin Coolidge's observation that "Persistence and determination alone are omnipotent." You can only be sure of losing when you give up. With so much at stake, it may be an immutable fact that going the extra mile is the only way to go.

Get big fast

4

IF THERE IS ONE COMPANY that embodies "get big fast," it is Cisco Systems. In 2000, Cisco completed 22 acquisitions and its revenues jumped to more than $18 billion in yet another record-breaking year. This was on top of 18 acquisitions in 1999, nine in 1998, and six in 1997. The company's 2000 earnings of over $2.7 billion exceed its total revenue as recently as 1995. Perhaps most incredible, Cisco is the market leader in 16 out of the 17 segments it serves. All this adds up to the fastest-growing and most profitable company in the history of the computer industry.

Since their beginnings, financial markets have rewarded scale. Investors are willing to pay a premium for a piece of success, and it isn't a small one. The leader in a market segment receives a valuation multiple that is several times that of its competitors. We live in a society that loves winners and is willing to pay them accordingly.

The concept of might makes right is also a self-fulfilling prophecy—the bigger a company becomes the greater its ability to grow. At Cisco, a passionate focus on growth launched its aggressive acquisition strategy. As competitors or attractive new products surfaced, Cisco was able to use its favorably valued equity to acquire them. Since market value is a function of share price multiplied by shares outstanding, the issuance of new shares for these purchases increased the value of Cisco, which would, in turn, make it easier for the company to acquire its next target, and so on and so on. For a brief period, Cisco was the most highly valued company in the world, with a market capitalization in excess of such stalwarts as General Electric, General Motors, and Microsoft. Even today, after a fairly significant pullback in the NASDAQ, the company remains one of the world's most valuable.

Getting big fast is by no means a concept unique to the high-technology world. Under the leadership of Jack Welch, General Electric became one of the most aggressive acquirers in the history of business. In 1999 alone, GE purchased a mind-boggling 134 companies. This represents an acquisition every 1.5 business days. "We'll go anywhere for an idea," said Welch. "When there are no limits to whom you'll see, where you'll go, what you'll touch, the results are remarkable. Everywhere we go, someone is doing something better." The rewards to GE's shareholders have been clear: The company's split adjusted share price has soared 4,500 percent since Welch took over. And in 2000, the *Financial Times* named General Electric as the world's most admired company.

Scale is essential for most companies, as the pace of change and growth today is driven not only by the desires of a given company's board of directors or its management but by external factors. In particular, as competition expands, many market leaders accelerate actions to maintain leadership. The sheer advantage of being able to outmuscle your market rivals makes size so important that boards and managers seize any opportunity for leadership. The impetus is often external, such as a competitor's smart move that inspires you to conceive an even smarter response. Some managers make entire careers as counterpunchers, one-upping the competition. Indeed, a company's growth may be dictated as much by its quick response to outside forces as by its own thought-out plans. Time Warner's acquisition of CNN in 1996 was a bold move by CEO Gerry Levin that subjected both him and the company to significant pressure. Yet, in hindsight it is admired as a deal that provided Time Warner a critical platform in the burgeoning cable industry. The company saw a market segment developing and, as it did with HBO, quickly reached out to capture an industry leader. Time Warner has consistently met the challenges of the market and today remains the largest media company in the world.

The Internet, almost by definition, shouts, "Get big fast." A commercial vehicle for just five years, this new medium has grown like no other. From a base of a few thousand users in the early nineties to hundreds of millions of global users today, the Web has taken root and soared to seemingly endless heights. And despite the fact that it has no history, no established models, and no order, it has rewarded those that have been able to cover ground fast and turn opportunities into solid businesses.

Like any radically new market, the Internet has a gold-rush aura, with prospectors racing to stake the first and biggest claim. Here, the rush is to stake the biggest market share by rapidly outgrowing your competitors. The companies that survived the NASDAQ crash were the ones that offered category leadership, enormous reach, or both. Emerging models, start-ups, and second-tier players watched their values plumet to such low

levels that it became difficult or impossible to execute a get-big-fast strategy. The Globe.com, for instance, saw its value decline from $1.6 billion to less than $20 million in early 2001, and iVillage, once worth more than $3.4 billion, has fallen to as low as $25 million in market capitalization. Without cash or highly valued equity, smaller players just didn't have the means to accelerate growth.

For winners such as Lycos, AOL, Yahoo!, Amazon, and e-Bay, it was critical to grow fast and establish market share before someone else snapped up the opportunity. In the early days, that kind of preemptive action was relatively easy; now it would be quite difficult. Attempting to build a new Web portal, or establish an online bookstore or auction business probably wouldn't be a good use of capital. Indeed, it would be foolhardy. The companies that plunged into the fray early and aggressively were able to develop impenetrable positions, leaving the early winners—the gold rush's skilled prospectors—still able to acquire and grow. They then had the means and the methods to defend their positions.

As mentioned, markets always pay a substantial premium for the leader in any field. Being a leader is important to investors, customers, and the talented people you want to hire. Leaders find themselves in a positive, self-reinforcing spiral. The bigger you are, the more people want to do business with you. And the more people want to do business with you, the bigger you get. Soon you have your competition at a disadvantage. But in order to achieve this position, it is essential to move fast.

There are no absolute answers when it comes to developing a growth strategy. What works for one management team may not work for another, and what works in one industry, such as textiles, for instance, may be completely inappropriate in another, such as technology. There are, however, some guiding principles and key strategies that every company and manager should consider.

< START WITH CUSTOMERS >

Later in this book, I'll discuss the importance of customers in great detail and will explain the many different constituencies that a business must appeal to. It's important to note, however, that any concept of growth, any notion of expansion, or any vision of scale must begin with one basic ingredient: the customer.

I'm amazed at how many executives lose sight of this immutable fact. While IBM is currently facing some Internet challenges, not that long ago the company's very survival seemed tenuous. Its stock was in a free fall, customers were jumping ship for newer and more efficient technologies, and, for the first time ever, IBM was laying off employees. But over the next few years the company pulled off one of the most dramatic turnarounds in business history. It implemented a strategy that lit a fire under staid old Big Blue. The result was remarkable growth. And how did the people at IBM do it? By getting close to customers, understanding their requirements, and working hard to fill them.

Lou Gerstner, IBM's CEO, once told *Business Week* magazine: "I came here with a view that you start your day with customers, that you start thinking about a company around its customers, and you organize around customers."

< EARLY IS ALWAYS EASIER THAN LATER >

A key part of our success at Lycos was our obsession with growth. We were barely four months old when we completed our first acquisition: In November of 1995, we purchased Point Communications in an all-stock transaction. And it wasn't long thereafter that I had some preliminary discussions with Yahoo!'s co-founder Jerry Yang about our companies working together. Our mutual goal was better leverage against Netscape, and how it positioned our companies on its pages. These conversations resulted in a meeting between Tim Koogle, Yahoo!'s newly hired CEO, Dave Wetherell, and myself at which Dave casually floated the idea of a merger between Lycos and Yahoo!.

It didn't take long to break the ice at the meeting—as we were sitting down, Dave, deep in conversation, tumbled backward over his chair and ended up on the floor. It gave us all a laugh, but you can't base a merger on a laugh. At that time, both companies' respective futures were looking pretty good, and, as a result, the dialogue never went very far.

A short time later, Lycos completed its public offering, and, for the next two years, we spent a lot more time thinking about earnings than we did about getting big fast. As I will note again and again in this book, I'm all for making money, but it's a fine line if profit is the only goal in a rapidly expanding market. Growth has got to be a big part of the equation. You have to find a healthy balance and stick with it.

< EQUITY IS A CURRENCY >

A large shareholder once told me that our stock, if used properly, was a license to print money. She was referring to the methods I outlined when describing Cisco: using equity to acquire market share. Basically, we were in a position to purchase any company with a valuation at or below our own, using nothing more than new shares of Lycos to pay for it. If the acquisitions were savvy, one that our shareholders could see as accretive during a reasonable period of time, our stock price would go up despite the fact that we were issuing new shares.

The result was that we would own a new business, our share price would increase, our shares outstanding would increase, our cash position would often improve due to the cash on hand of the company we acquired, and our market capitalization would typically jump by a good deal more than we'd paid for the business. In essence, the acquisition was free. Over the long term, we would need to deliver back to the market in terms of earnings per share, but, in the short run, we were being paid handsomely for growing. Once I understood this model, I felt as if I'd been handed the means to get big fast. Now the question became where to use it.

Yet I woke up one day in the middle of 1997, when Lycos was about two years old, and saw a world I didn't like. In any given month, we reached roughly 14 percent of Internet users. Yahoo!, by comparison, had an audience reach of 50 to 55 percent. Other competitors, such as Infoseek and Excite, also had substantially greater audiences than we did.

It was obvious what we needed to do. Pursue a strategy of aggressive acquisitions.

<BUY MARKET SHARE>

The equity-based approach I described above made me quite anxious. Understanding it intellectually and putting it into practice were two different things. We had just become profitable: How could we start buying early-stage companies and remain so? I remember calling the chief executive of one of the investment banks that had put together our public offering. I described my misgivings about going back to a negative bottom line. He said I was right—our market valuation would suffer. He added a warning: If I were to buy a company that diluted our earnings, it would be the last company I acquired—Wall Street wouldn't give us the currency to do it again.

Fortunately, I overcame my trepidation and ignored his cautionary advice. Shortly afterward, we made our first significant acquisition, purchasing Tripod for $58 million in February 1998. As the Web's leading community site, Tripod transformed Lycos. Suddenly, we became so much more than a search site offering features that stood out from those of our competitors; our sustainable differentiation was under way.

We made the decision after intense research on the market segments and businesses that had the potential to change Lycos' competitive landscape. We focused especially on the concept of community, which I see as the essence of the Web. By fully engaging the user, the Web eliminates passivity and elicits an active response that connects millions of people with other people. It is talk-with computing. By contrast, other media create not lively participants but mute recipients—couch potatoes. Think of the words we use to designate a person who "views" or "listens to" television and one who "uses" the Internet. The connotations are clear.

When we were shopping for a partner, this sense of the Web as a global neighborhood was uppermost in my mind. So we went looking for a community-oriented company, one with rapid organic growth, where users literally create the content and become part of it. We spoke with many sites, including Geocities, Angelfire, Fortune City, Xoom, and Tripod.

Tripod quickly became our focus. It had numerous advantages, not the least of which was the fact that it was the only company based in Massachusetts, where we had our headquarters. Given this was to be our first real test at integrating two companies, I felt the local proximity would serve us well. When I first met Tripod's two founders, they turned out to be a remarkably impressive duo who embodied the free spirit of the Internet: Bo Peabody, a recent college graduate; and Dick Sabot, his professor, who also happened to be a world-class economist and a distinguished author.

Tripod had virtually no revenue, but it was generating users—lots of them. In July 1997, Ted Philip and I arranged to meet Peabody and Sabot. Driving from opposite directions across Massachusetts, we met in a diner at about ten o'clock at night. The four of us sat down and began to share our thoughts and visions. It was a very exciting meeting as ideas poured out, and we realized that we were all on the same wavelength—and could barely contain our enthusiasm for the Web's future. Over the next few weeks, we negotiated a term sheet, a price, and a strategy. All we needed were the signatures.

Then the process unraveled. We were so timid about getting the deal done that we had violated the rule of speed by allowing other suitors time to arrive.

In September 1997, we had a very sad and disappointing call from Tripod: They were signing a no-shop agreement preliminary to selling the company to America Online. I was devastated. Ours was a merger that made sense: Our cultures fit, the product was a match for our users, and the price was right. We had all the ingredients except the deal itself.

This was clearly a lesson learned in the merger-and-acquisition business. Success, after a certain level of due diligence, requires lightning-fast execution. Once the terms are agreed to, the dynamics are straightforward. A buyer needs to close the deal as quickly as possible to avoid the mess we found ourselves in. On the other hand, a seller wants to delay the process just long enough to shop the offer to other potential buyers. Any investment bank worth its salt can test the market for competing offers in days or even hours. It's simple: "Here's my offer, can you beat it?"

But the game hadn't quite ended. AOL was preoccupied with other deals and its maturing Virginia culture didn't match the T-shirt, shorts, and sandals found at Tripod. The no-shop agreement ran out in mid-December, and I received a phone call from Tripod's adviser, Morgan Stanley, asking if we were we still interested in the company. Despite that fact that I harbored some of the anger of a lover scorned, we agreed that further talks were worthwhile, provided we could resolve things quickly. Both sides had other deals in the works.

At about four o'clock in the afternoon of December 30, 1997, we met at Lycos, determined to outline an agreement and negotiate its terms. By eleven o'clock that night, we still had a long way to go, and it was suggested that we knock off and resume the next day, New Year's Eve. But I was adamant: We would either stay and negotiate through the night or Lycos would pull out of the deal. So negotiate we did, until about eleven o'clock the next morning, when we finally signed a term sheet and agreed to buy Tripod—our first significant acquisition.

We came to it with focus, determination, and luck—all built on a foundation of methodical and rigorous research. We quickly began a torrid shopping spree. Acquiring nine more companies, we built up a network of sites and vaulted into the top category of Web destinations. We had found, in the words of Austin Powers, our mojo.

Lycos quickly evolved into a multibrand network, a change born not of opportunity but of necessity. Having defined ourselves as a media business, we had to become a credible player in that category. We knew that all large media companies operate across numerous brands. The reasoning is that no matter how good you are, no matter how strong your product is, no one brand can reach all potential readers, viewers, listeners, or users. The world is too diverse. There are too many niche demographics out there.

Viacom, for example, owns a variety of TV brands, among them CBS, MTV, VH1, Comedy Central, and Nickelodeon, and a host of other brands in the publishing and film industries. Disney owns multiple film-production studios, including Miramax and Touchstone, along with ABC and ESPN, theme parks, and a variety of cable and print assets. Time Warner, the biggest of them all, is perhaps the most diverse. It owns the magazines *Time, Fortune, People, Money, Sports Illustrated,* and many others, each with its own distinct audience, plus the cable giants CNN and HBO, and the moviemaker Warner Brothers, among others. And now America Online has bought Time Warner, further extending the reach of both companies. By constantly segmenting their audiences, either demographically or by interest type, big media companies inevitably grow bigger faster than a single-brand company ever could.

This realization was an epiphany for us. Gearing up for growth in February 1998, we went about buying companies to acquire their brands, their audience, and their talented employee base. And in October 1998, we rolled out the Lycos network.

Our network was extensive, reached many segments of the market, and had a huge audience. Content included Tripod, HotBot, Wired News, WhoWhere? AngelFire, Matchmaker, Gamesville, and many others. Each brand maintained its independence. We then worked hard to show the market that, like Time Warner, Lycos was a well-designed network and not a gaggle of stragglers with no coherent purpose. We followed the television model and used each of our properties to drive users to the others, thereby making the entire network stronger.

If you watch any half hour of prime-time television, you'll see promotions for other shows on the same network. The networks use their successful programming to build awareness of the less-watched shows—the popular products strengthen the struggling ones. We learned to do the same thing online: Lycos promotes HotBot; HotBot promotes Tripod; Tripod promotes Gamesville; and so on.

The results have been remarkable. Our market value soared from less than $400 million, when our network began, to a peak of over $9 billion. Our audience reach of 14 percent in 1997 soared to over 50 percent by 1999. By any definition, we had arrived at the pinnacle of the new media market.

And we kept acquiring companies. We understood that our fundamental asset was our ability to build a large audience and then sell that audience to whoever who wanted to communicate with it, namely advertisers. So we kept looking for ways to bring in companies that would further extend our reach. We analyzed how they would overlap with our current audience and if they would enable us to reach a new demographic. If we determined they could add value, we went after them aggressively.

There were no hard-and-fast criteria for acquisitions. At a minimum, any company we acquired needed a sound brand, a strong employee base, and, most important, good audience momentum. We also kept multiple balls in the air, recognizing that we needed a choice of many more companies than we could acquire in order to pinpoint the relative few that promised genuine opportunity.

For every company we acquired, we looked at perhaps ten other possibilities. A given target might fall through for any number of reasons—we weren't comfortable with the company's management, they didn't like us, its finances didn't stand up to close examination, we didn't love the product, we couldn't reach agreement on a price or terms, or simply that they ultimately decided not to sell their company. But we kept looking.

At that point, we were very focused on growth. In fact, the theme of the presentation and discussion at our board of directors meeting just prior to our buying spree was "get big fast." We didn't have much to lose; after all, at that time we were small and very much in danger of becoming irrelevant in a crowded Internet field. We had already made the mistake of focusing solely on internal growth through all of 1996 and half of 1997. We weren't going to let any more time pass. Even I was surprised by how quickly we narrowed the gap.

We became quite adept at picking up properties at reasonable prices. I credit this to our sense of timing concerning emerging trends. We looked for companies on the cusp of their full potential. For instance, we paid just $58 million for Tripod; less than a year later Yahoo! acquired Tripod's biggest competitor, Geocities, for $4 billion. Our acquisition list was extensive and included Gamesville, which we bought at the height of the Internet bubble for $248 million in stock. We paid $542,000 for Point; $69 million for Quote.com, a leading finance site; $45 million for Matchmaker, a dating site; $49 million for Sonique, an MP3 music player; $159 million for WhoWhere, a network of sites ranging from personal publishing to white pages; and $290 million for Wired Digital, which included the HotBot search engine and the much-acclaimed Wired News and its team of technology journalists. All totaled, our acquisitions—which netted us nearly 35 points of user reach—cost less than $860 million. By comparison, some competitors with total reach of less than 35 percent were trading at market values of billions of dollars.

<GET GLOBAL FAST>

The global economy has developed like a firestorm. Over the last three years, with ever-increasing frequency, leading national players in the United States and other countries are waking up to find themselves bit players on the world stage. This has led to a rash of international mergers. Terra Lycos was the first on the Internet, yet across a myriad of industries, global alliances have been taking place at unprecedented speed. New polyglot names abound, such as the Credit Suisse First Boston, recent acquisition of Donaldson, Lufkin and Jenrette, blurring everyone's antecedents in the process. What nationality is Daimler Benz Chrysler or Deutsche Telecom Voicestream? Who knows, and does it matter? Hewlett-Packard's Carly Fiorina has good advice for all of us: "Think global. Think borderless. Think interdependent. Think interconnected."

You could add, "Think deep." Globalization's opportunities are not necessarily what they appear to be at first glance. For example, U.S. companies initially assumed that the world's consumers are now so alike that millions covet the same things. (This is the Americanized World theory that sparks charges of U.S. "cultural imperialism.") By this logic, U.S. companies could simply export their domestic processes and enjoy economies of scale abroad.

Reality is more interesting. The world may devour U.S. movies, music, and jeans, but cultures remain profoundly different in terms of religion, language, politics, education, and other fundamental beliefs. Accordingly, the big U.S. opportunities may have less to do with selling American culture and consumer goods than with leveraging the Internet—the new U.S. infrastructure—and exporting information technology in ways that truly globalize the Internet as a medium shared by all cultures. By this perspective, global business opportunities lie in leveraging economies of knowledge and expanding information media for all cultures, however different.

At Lycos, our international presence was long a point of successful differentiation. It was in May 1996, with the company still less than a year old, that we began our relationship with German media giant Bertelsmann. This alliance, which started as a technology-license agreement for Germany, quickly expanded into a broad pan-European venture responsible for the launch of local-language Lycos sites in a dozen countries. To this day, Lycos maintains operations in more European countries than any competitor, and Lycos Europe is itself a publicly traded company on German's Neur Markt.

Bertelsmann, the most global of media companies with 600 businesses in 54 countries, including Doubleday, the publisher of this book, has proven to be an exceptional partner. In fact, Thomas Middelhoff, as Bertelsmann's CEO, was a key broker in the Terra Lycos merger, committing $1 billion in advertising purchases over the next five years, along with the use of Bertelsmann's extensive content library.

With Europe as a foundation, we quickly duplicated our joint-venture model around the world. We introduced Lycos Japan in 1998 with three partners: Sumitomo, a $100-billion-per-year conglomerate; Kadakowa Shoten, a large Japanese publisher; and Internet Initiative Japan, the country's largest Internet service provider. Lycos Korea was rolled out with Mirae, a Korean electronics company, and was quickly followed by a $50-million joint venture with Singapore Telecom for the balance of Asia, which at present includes Lycos in Mainland China, Malaysia, Thailand, Taiwan, Hong Kong, India, and Singapore, among others. The most recent agreement was a $60-million partnership with Bell Canada that created the country's leading Web portal.

All of these agreements have had the same purpose—rapid expansion financed by strong local partners, offering significant value through revenue diversification. We knew, of course, that there was a downside to these joint ventures: We were sacrificing a degree of control and giving up a percentage of our company. Someone else now owned a piece of Lycos Europe and Lycos Japan, and, as a result, we were unable to consolidate their revenue on our income statements and unilaterally direct their strategies.

On the up side, our joint ventures built great value. Even in countries where we didn't understand the culture, the people, the products, or the language, we were able to find partners who could get a service up and running for us. We selected companies, not individuals, and together we staffed organizations with people who understood local markets. We were able to build a good product not only quickly but also efficiently and effectively.

The outcome of our strategy was that Lycos became a global leader. The company is now number one in Canada, number two behind Yahoo! in Japan, number one in Korea, and a leader across Europe, with very strong positions in Scandinavia, Germany, and France. In all, we established Lycos in 27 countries. We built a joint-venture employee base outside of the United States of over 2,000. And now with the Terra Lycos merger complete, the company has the broadest reach of any Internet company, operating in 41 countries, nearly double the number of our nearest competitor. And it came about only because we focused on growing global fast and doing it in a big way.

< GET LOCAL FAST >

Yes, new global enterprises continue to appear every day, but business leaders are learning the absolute necessity of local market execution. You need smart people on the ground who understand the culture, context, and relationships of a market. You can't just airlift in a team from the U.S. and expect them to impose your way of doing things on a foreign culture.

It makes no sense to dictate local decisions from the other side of the globe. This is the lesson learned the hard way by colonial powers such as the British Empire, which began unraveling with the Boston Tea Party and suffered subsequent rebellions from India to Ireland, until the sun that never set on the empire did just that.

Global companies need strong local management teams who understand business and cultural customs, product preference, distribution networks, and scores of other subtleties. Yes, money talks, but not always clearly enough to pierce the mysterious barriers between this very big world's diverse peoples.

So a global company needs lots of local help. GE's Jack Welch has coined the term "boundaryless thinking" to describe his own approach to globalization. He sees GE as having a global culture, which means that management should stop assuming there is any "one right way" to do things. Instead, the home office becomes a clearinghouse for sharing best practices and processes across the board. What works well for GE in Asia, for example, will be examined for possible export to Germany, and what works well in Germany may prove useful in the United States.

In formulating your own approach, you might look at the long history of The Coca-Cola Company, once the world's most ubiquitous business, truly "global" before the word became fashionable. By the 1950s, Coca-Cola was surely the world champion of decentralized control, with the company's Atlanta headquarters having successfully delegated genuine authority and responsibility to Coke's global network of local bottling companies. These businesses were free to operate in response to local conditions, and the overall company thrived. As Coke's current chairman, Douglas Daft, recently put it, "We succeeded in building a company that was global in scope because we avoided managing it as a global company."

But in the mid-1980s, Coca-Cola began to centralize by consolidating independent bottlers in response to an increasingly consolidated retail environment. The surviving network of larger bottlers was more efficient, cut costs, and delighted Coke shareholders. By the early 1990s, Coca-Cola exemplified globalization as it was then defined and *Fortune* extolled it as the "world's best brand."

Suddenly the situation changed. As Daft recalls, "A very real backlash developed ... which in hindsight was predictable, natural, and relatively healthy. Local governments and individuals responded with a renewed zeal for keeping control over their local politics, local culture, and local products. The very forces that were making the world more connected and more homogeneous were simultaneously triggering a desire to preserve what was uniquely local."

No longer the good guys they always thought they were, Coke's managers had to reempower local bottlers. At the same time, they had to strengthen the company's global competitiveness. The result is a potent mix of central management and local autonomy not unlike Jack Welch's prescription for GE.

"We are not simply giving up global for local," says Daft. "We are enhancing our ability to operate locally from our solid global base." Basically, this means cultivating close relationships with local bottlers and retailers in 200 countries and 126 languages—a trust- and talent-building campaign.

"If you ask me what our business is," says Daft, "my answer is pretty simple. Every day, we either enrich or erode the billions of relationships required for our business to succeed. . . . In every country, our workforce must truly represent the local society—not because it's politically correct . . . but because the very nature of our business requires that kind of diverse insight and perspective to really flourish."

<VIEW JOINT VENTURES AS A VALUE VEHICLE>

Joint ventures are solid when each party offers a set of complementary assets. In Japan, for instance, Lycos had the products while Sumitomo had the cash and local market expertise.

But there's considerable risk, and alliances often fail—and it's not hard to see why. How to share control, provide funding, deal with dilution, diversification, and commitments from management are just some of the issues that have to be negotiated. Our model has been successful because we developed a clear-cut set of objectives and guidelines, and adhered to them.

Less predictable, alas, is that nagging intangible—chemistry between management teams. Unforeseen fiascos like the dismal

DaimlerChrysler impasse, pitting Prussian owners against Detroit managers, attest to the absolute imperative of scouting the emotional landscape before making the financial commitment. "In business as in marriage," notes Dick Sabot, "it's a terrible mistake to marry for money alone. You have to make sure that there's genuine shared affection and a common goal."

<USE YOUR BOARD OF DIRECTORS>

A properly assembled board of directors can be a tremendous asset to any business. Consider how rich those lifetimes of experience are. Derive the most value from your board. Excite demonstrated the power of this strategy: It built business alliances with Netscape, Intuit, and AOL, all of which were inspired by the common affiliations of their board members. From the bankers of Hong Kong to the brokers of London's City to the jewelers of Zurich, there's an age-old reason for alliances based on de facto family relationships. It can be boiled down to trust. Despite all folk wisdom to the contrary, it pays to do business with friends—the right friends.

<DON'T BE TOO GREEDY>

Knowing how to identify good and great deals without mandating lopsided victories is a requirement for any good negotiator. Countless Web companies have missed opportunities by awaiting valuations that were unrealistic. Less than 12 months ago, we were rebuffed after offering a company several hundred million dollars for its business. Then the markets dried up and so did our offer. That company was liquidated in January 2001. It held out too long and lost everything.

The buyer must adhere to this principle with equal diligence. Many deals evaporate because aggressive purchasers try to browbeat their targets. We did that with a store hosting company with which we had signed a letter of intent to purchase about the same time as we were buying Tripod. Our due diligence showed a few challenges, all of which could have been worked around. Yet we used those challenges as an opportunity to drive the price down. We reached an impasse, only to have a competitor purchase the company a few weeks later for a substantial premium to our price. The company then became the basis for its e-commerce efforts. The price, within reason, should have been irrelevant. We became too greedy and we lost.

"You especially have to worry about arrogance," Marc Andreessen, chairman and co-founder of Loudcloud, Inc., noted not long ago. "If everyone is telling you you're succeeding—your stock price is up, your customers are paying you, everything is going great—you start to believe you're succeeding because you're brilliant and everything you do in the future will be brilliant. That's when you start to make serious mistakes."

< THE BIG MISTAKE >

As far back as 1997, I was concerned with the sense of irrational euphoria that had developed around our industry. That concern grew in the years that followed as the NASDAQ continued to reach new highs while the companies listed on it continued to show greater losses. Now, to be clear, I remained at all times a firm believer in the profound impact the Internet would have on both our society and economy for decades to come. Further, it was clear that during that period we were witnessing the formation of some powerful companies. By 1999, however, it was equally clear that the market had reached a stage of temporary insanity with multibillion-dollar valuations being assigned to companies that had neither revenue nor earnings.

The drive to build a company that deserved its market valuation was uppermost in my mind. It was for this reason that I became very excited when Barry Diller, Chairman and CEO of USA Networks, called me in the first days of February 1999 to propose combining portions of our companies.

Several months preceding his call, Dave Wetherell, the chairman of CMGI, who at the time owned roughly 20 percent of Lycos, had decided that he wanted to diversify his holdings and had asked me to begin looking for a strategic partner who might purchase some or all of his shares. As a result, I had conversations with nearly every major media company in the United States. I met some extremely intelligent and forward-thinking executives and gained new insight about which traditional-media assets would be most beneficial to Lycos. Equally important, I learned which of our assets would help them.

I had always regarded Barry as both a powerful executive and a media visionary. His career accomplishments read like few others—vice president of Primetime Television for ABC Entertainment; chairman and chief executive officer of television shopping icon QVC; chairman and chief executive officer of Fox; and for ten years, chairman of the board of directors of Paramount Pictures. The idea of teaming with a man who had accomplished so much held great appeal for me.

My excitement increased after we sat down to discuss the framework of his proposal in February 1999. He suggested that we combine all of Lycos with certain of USA's assets. We would receive all of the Home Shopping Network, its million square feet of warehouse space, its 60 million cable households, its 2,000-person call center, and its $1 billion in annual sales. Further, we would receive all of TicketMaster, the nation's ticketing behemoth, and all of USA's Internet assets. Finally, we would merge in the assets of TicketMaster CitySearch, a public company in its own right and the leader in the rapidly growing field of local content and commerce.

Despite the fact that up until this point I was fiercely committed to Lycos' independence, the combination was just too good to pass up. All told, Barry Diller was willing to merge assets that generated over $1 billion in revenue and nearly $300 million a year in earnings, at a time when Lycos' revenues during its entire existence didn't total $300 million. In addition, my conversations with other media executives convinced me that it was going to be difficult to place Wetherell's shares. Whoever I spoke to, the story was always the same: "We will trade advertising for a piece of your company, but we will not use cash to buy it." These executives were surely believers in the medium and desperately wanted to own a piece of it. They simply could not justify the multiples and sought any means but cash or stock to budge their way in.

In the meantime, I increasingly felt we were on the edge of a bubble in Internet values that could burst at any time. The USA deal would give us a floor with real earnings and huge assets. More important, we would be creating a first-of-a-kind powerhouse—a company that combined old-economy assets with new-economy excitement. The Home Shopping Network's distribution expertise would enable us to build a mega-portal that offered consumers the best of a Yahoo!, Lycos, and Amazon all rolled into one.

Our board of directors moved judiciously. They methodically analyzed my presentation of the deal, and then heard from lawyers, accountants, and investment bankers. In the end, the vote in support of the merger was unanimous. I'll never forget the pride I felt when Dave Wetherell stood up after the vote and led a round of applause. He called the merger a "watershed event for the industry that will forever transform the way Internet deals get done." I was elated—and never would have believed that just 24 hours later all hell would break loose.

We announced the merger on the morning of Tuesday, February 9, 1999. Then the stock crashed. The deal was complex and, more than that, I had overestimated the financial markets' willingness to accept a merger between our high-growth new-economy assets and the traditional businesses of USA. No one believed they needed to embrace this revolutionary union; after all, Internet stocks could do no wrong. Just look at a few of the news headlines in the weeks leading up to the announcement:

At the close of markets that Tuesday, Lycos stock was off some 26 percent, with CMGI close behind with a 14-percent drop.

Bad quickly became worse. Dave Wetherell, who had backed me so strongly earlier in the week, appeared to panic with the drop in stock value. In his conversations with the press he wavered in his support and, by the end of the day on February 11, our death knell was posted on the CMGI Web site: "CMGI is generally supportive of the deal, but reserves the right to reassess its position as developments unfold." With these few words, he had made it clear that his support was far from certain.

The deal was dead 48 hours after we announced it. From that moment on, the story was never about strategy or vision. It was a story about Dave Wetherell defending the honor and purity of Internet stocks against the villainous Barry Diller, who had dared suggest that old media had a role in this new world *The Wall Street Journal*'s headline on the controversy said it all: TV TITAN AND WEB MASTER BATTLE OVER LYCOS.

While Wetherell was becoming a folk hero, I was being vilified. Some reporters managed to do both in the same story. On February 11, 1999—the same day that Wetherell delivered the fatal blow on the CMGI Web site—James Cramer, the celebrated hedge-fund manager, CNBC commentator, and principal behind financial information TheStreet.com wrote the following:

> CMGI WON'T BE TAKEN UNDER
>
> In a flabbergasting turn, CMGI, the big Lycos shareholder, isn't going for this "take under." Net bulls should rejoice. The hijacking of Lycos by someone from that slick, old Hollywood crowd, that computer illiterate group of nonbelievers, may be busted!

The biggest sea change in the Net was not so much that Lycos' Bob Davis got seduced by the attractiveness of going Hollywood, but that CMGI, some of the toughest minds in the Net business, were willing to go along. Frankly, this frightened the heck out of me. I had this vision of Lycos' network being worth a heck of a lot more than Diller's. Diamonds to zirconium doesn't cut it in my books . . . The only thing more stupid than merging with Home Shopping would be to go into the catalog industry!

I was becoming the Antichrist to many individual investors who refused to believe any scenario that did not feature Internet stocks soaring into the stratosphere. And just as rapidly as my reputation was fading, Wetherell's star was ascending.

I became increasingly frustrated at the course of events. Not only because the deal's chances were fading, but also because I wasn't being given an opportunity to outline our vision. No one wanted to hear about the great new company we were creating. Shareholders were fascinated with the concept of Wetherell masterminding a topping offer and refused to focus on the potential of USA Lycos. The media certainly wasn't interested in our proposed company: The saga of "Barry vs. Dave" made much better copy.

On numerous occasions, I had asked, cajoled, and even begged Wetherell to stop the saber rattling just long enough to give me an opportunity to pitch the deal in an environment that would allow the market to listen. I remember especially well investment banker Hambrecht and Quist's annual technology conference that year. Held in the mountain resort of Snowbird, Utah, it was very friendly territory. H&Q was a key member of our IPO underwriting team, and their Internet equity analyst, Paul Noglows, had long been one of our strongest supporters. He had even raised Lycos' rating to the firm's highest—"strong buy"—

based on the merits of the proposed merger. If ever there was an opportunity to convince Wetherell to budge, this was it.

I had no such luck. I was rebuffed over and over again. As time passed, he only became more emboldened, ultimately resigning from our board of directors on March 9 and hiring Morgan Stanley to help him search for alternatives to the merger, with one possibility being CMGI itself purchasing Lycos.

I felt betrayed. The hard work of the Lycos team had created tremendous wealth for both Dave Wetherell personally and for CMGI. We were now left hanging out to dry. All the while, Dave reiterated to me that it was all about business, and that he still had tremendous respect for my leadership. The test of those sentiments came quickly. The *Boston Globe* was planning a profile on my career. They desperately wanted a quote from Wetherell about my skills, background, business acumen, anything. The story, a very positive one by and large, ran on March 23, 1999, without a word from CMGI. Wetherell wrote me an e-mail explaining that he had been on vacation and too busy to talk with the press, even though he continued to dialogue with news organizations across the country. More than any of his actions, this was the one that hit me the hardest. Feeling hurt on a very personal level, perhaps more so than at any time in my career, I knew exactly what I had to do next.

It became clear the deal wasn't going to happen. We needed 50.1 percent of the outstanding shareholders to vote in favor of the merger, and the math wasn't in our favor. I presented this reality at a USA board of directors meeting, explaining that CMGI's 20 percent, along with the 25 percent of shareholders who traditionally don't vote, meant we would need to receive almost 95 percent of the remaining ballots to complete the merger. (Our bylaws stated that any shareholder who failed to return a proxy card, for any reason, would be considered a vote against.) This was a powerful board that included Diller; General Norman Schwarzkopf; Edgar Bronfman, CEO of Seagram's; and Paul Allen, of Microsoft fame. Everyone quickly saw that there was little hope.

Under the terms of the merger agreement, Barry Diller could have forced the issue to a shareholder vote. He would have had nothing to lose by doing so, and the earliest possible vote would have been six months hence. I knew, however, that six months of uncertainty risked destroying the company. Barry agreed, and, on May 10, 1999, only three months after rolling out our grand vision of old and new economies rushing together, we announced the termination of our merger plans.

I completed the usual circuit of business television shows on the morning after the announcement and, on my trip back to the office, was informed that Wetherell was urgently trying to reach me. He told me that CMGI wanted to buy Lycos. Despite my misgivings, he still owned 20 percent of the company, and I reluctantly agreed to meet. It quickly became apparent that he hoped to buy Lycos at a price lower than that at the time of our USA announcement, the same deal he had been so vociferously criticizing as being too low.

I was flabbergasted. After appropriate board consultation, I informed Dave that we weren't interested and that Lycos needed some time to focus on just being Lycos.

Unwilling to accept our refusal, he warned over a dinner meeting that he might take a hostile offer to the market. I encouraged him to do so if he didn't mind my telling the market that I considered CMGI grossly overvalued. We reached a tense impasse, and he went away, as did this entire ugly mess. Lycos moved on.

In a final irony from this difficult period, it was Diller, the supposed saboteur of Internet value, who selflessly released Lycos from the merger in the best interests of our business. He showed genuine concern for both me and my company. It was my friend Wetherell, who so endlessly worked to kill a merger that just days before he had so enthusiastically endorsed, who made the big mistake. By denying me the opportunity to discuss the merits of the deal, he deprived the market of any chance to consider a merger of old- and new-economy companies nearly a year before the AOL and Time Warner combination.

Postscript: By early 2001, CMGI stock had plunged from a high of $163 per share to less than $5, a loss of more than 97 percent, with its market value falling by tens of billions to just over $1.4 billion. At the same time, TheStreet.com, publisher of so many damning articles about the merger, was down to $65 million in value, from at one point, more than $1.6 billion. On December 10, 2000, the *New York Times* reported, "CMGI is closing other units, laying off employees, and facing tough questions about the viability of the business behind the flashing lights and New Economy rhetoric."

I still regret the failure of that deal, partly because the logic underlying it was so strong. It would have allowed us to get big fast. It was the same logic that drove the merger between AOL and Time Warner a year later. Both companies were rapidly expanding into new areas: Time Warner into the online world and AOL into traditional media. I'm told that while they were negotiating, the AOL and Time Warner people had whiteboards full of the details of the USA-Lycos agreement. I felt vindicated. The markets have struggled with the AOL Time Warner merger as well, but I have no doubt it will prove to be brilliant. It combines a powerful set of assets with an exceptional management team. In five years, their stockholders are going to be very happy.

< SEIZE THE FUTURE >

After our deal failed, I felt like an early explorer who claimed new territory on the frontier, only to have it stolen. But, fortunately, we put our heads down, moved forward, and built an even stronger company. Attaining success in any business is complicated, but maintaining it long term is far more complex than the stock market is inclined to recognize. Yet success always begins in the same way: with a compelling vision that you are determined to transform into a thriving business. More rapidly than ever, companies are merging models, technologies, and concepts to achieve unprecedented scale. Media companies are buying telecommunications assets, Internet companies are buying old media, and, in the ultimate irony, a record company has invested in Napster. The race for scale and size has resulted in a giant whirlwind of activity.

The current playing field is not for the faint of heart. In the long run, however, it boils down to having a compelling vision that leads to growing revenues and consistent profitability. That involves knowing the marketplace, knowing your employees and competencies, and recognizing competitive threats and opportunities. It means spending wisely.

And in the twenty-first century, it means getting big fast.

It's all about brand

5

NOT LONG AGO, Don Keough, chairman of Allen & Company, told me about the importance of brand to The Coca-Cola Company, where he previously served as president. "Suppose," he told me, "that every asset of the company was destroyed—every building, truck, plant, bottle, can, vending machine, and sign. Now, the only thing left would be the trademark right of ownership, the brand, Coca-Cola. You could fill Yankee stadium with bankers from around the world willing to lend you whatever you needed to rebuild, based on the value of the brand."

In other words, it's all about the brand.

Many managers seem to think that brand refers only to how their products are defined and positioned. But that is not the case. Your brand evokes images and quickly conjures up a handful of words and associations that convey to anyone who sees it what the company is. It is the company's personality; it should make people feel favorably toward it. In this way, it positions the entire business for all of your relevant constituencies—not just customers, but actual and prospective employees, shareholders, suppliers, bankers, and competitors. Your brand is your company.

Lexus is an example of an outstanding automobile company: the quality of car, service, and advertising consistently convey the same message. If the Lexus brand has a certain aura that its marketers have created, so does Starbucks. It is more than a car or a cup of coffee. Starbucks offers an experience through its packaging, its knowledgeable salespeople, its retail environment, even its music and its oversized, comfortable chairs.

Though all great brands have in common a distinctive aura, those who create the brands are not necessarily any more alike than are the parents of musical prodigies. For example, the Lexus brand was midwifed by a Madison Avenue ad agency. Howard Schultz of Starbucks, on the other hand, couldn't afford advertising in those days and he built his brand in the only way open to him—letting Starbucks coffeehouses speak for themselves. And speak they did, each establishment creating a local ambience and local clientele that soon had a ripple effect all over the country. The result was one of the most valuable brands in existence. "We concentrated on creating value and customer service," Schultz once noted. "Our success proves you can build a national brand without 30-second sound bites. . . . It proves that the best way to build a brand is one customer at a time."

At the other end of the spectrum are marketers who manage to bring a once vibrant brand out of the doldrums into a whole new second life. Steve Jobs has done it with Apple computers and the wildly popular Mac of the 1980s, only to see the Apple brand nearly die after he left the company. Since his return, Jobs has revitalized Apple by, among other things, launching the imaginative iMac computers. These eye-catching machines combine lively appearance and performance in much the same ways that made the original Macs so appealing. Not only is the Apple brand reviving, but it turns out that iMac buyers are largely first-time computer users, just like the original Mac buyers.

Michael Eisner is another remarkable brand-saver. When he became chairman and chief executive officer of The Walt Disney Company in 1984, he breathed new life into that brand.

Today, Disney is a $23-billion empire so vast and diverse (animation blockbusters, three movie studios, two television networks, five theme parks, 757 stores, etc.) that it weathers financial storms with seeming ease. But even more important, Michael Eisner has revitalized the Disney brand by establishing a singularly productive tension between the company's commitment to squeaky-clean "good taste" and highly creative entertainments, such as the animation classics *Lion King* and *Beauty and the Beast.*

In the summer of 2000, I talked to Michael about a collaboration between Terra Lycos and Disney. Above all during our narrowly focused talks, he was committed to maintaining complete control over his brands. He was unwavering in this. In a recent interview in the *Harvard Business Review*, Eisner described neo-Disney culture as a kind of crucible where creative ideas deliberately clash with "common sense," the result being the Disney brand—an alloy of artistic excellence, commercial appeal, and moral purity. "The high road is often harder but more rewarding creatively," said Eisner. "Our brand is our greatest asset, and we handle it with extreme care." Eisner continued: "We think of a brand like a pointillist painting. Everything you do for your brand is a point on the canvas. An advertising campaign is one point, say. Each customer's experience is a point. The quality of a new CD-ROM is a point—an animated movie, a Broadway show, a new theme park, and so on. At the end of a decade, you can have hundreds and thousands of new, wonderful, pretty points, and they can create a beautiful brand picture. But if you've been sloppy with some of your points, you can have an atrophied, old-fashioned, muddled picture . . . A brand takes a long time to build, and a long time to destroy, and both happen as a result of lots and lots of small actions. If you want to be strong, each point along the way has to be as close to perfect as possible."

Defending your brand is about as close to a sacred duty as anything in business gets. Hewlett-Packard's Fiorina explains the reason why: "I believe that a brand is a promise to our customers and a reminder to ourselves of what we should stand for and who we should be." Paul Tagliabue, commissioner of the National Football League, put the same idea another way in a conversation with me. "Brand is vital across the board. As I see it, your brand has to be not only well recognized, but also very clear as to what it stands for. In our case, I think, the NFL brand stands for tradition, for passion, for integrity, for quality, and finally it stands for the league being greater than any of the individual teams. The whole is greater than the sum of its parts."

Clear commitment has driven the Lycos brand, too. We wanted it to convey directly and simply that our content would satisfy the customer's need to get deeply immersed in whatever it is that he or she feels passionately and intellectually curious about. For example, if music is your passion, we thought that Lycos Music offers rich and stimulating choices that will broaden your knowledge and enhance your taste. The same is true for games at Lycos Gamesville, and nearly every other interest a person could have. Whatever you are into, we wanted you to be able to pursue it more deeply on Lycos.

The process of branding—which includes creating, tending to, and defending your brand—is absolutely crucial to any successful operation. In fact, whether your company sells directly to consumers or to other businesses, brand is the essence of any business, and it should be at the core of its strategy. It is so critical that it presents one of the few exceptions to my general rule that speed is life. Branding cannot and should not be rushed. It is a work in progress that is never finished. Like success, branding isn't a destination; it is a journey that lasts for the life of the company. Since you will never complete it, you will work on it simultaneously with other tasks before you.

Branding must be accomplished with resolution and, above all, consistency. Regardless of the size of your budget, you have to make it a priority. It entails constantly repeating the same message, image, and story, and maintaining a steady marketing presence. When a company's advertising appears and disappears, it is wasted. It is impossible to build momentum with customers unless you make it a steady and constant process.

We looked at the 2000 Super Bowl for an example of the fiasco of one-shot advertising. Of the 55 Super Bowl advertisers, 18 were upstart dot.coms trying to gather an audience beyond Wall Street. Many used their entire advertising budgets (some used their IPO capital, too) on 30-second commercials, such as the now defunct pet.com's sock-puppet dog. Almost without exception, these and other forgettable spots sank without a trace. In an *Adweek* survey of 400 viewers after the game, only one out of three could even name a dot-com brand they saw advertised. According to *Forbes*, dot.coms spent roughly $50 million on Super Bowl spots and attracted some 1.1 million additional visitors to their sites as a result. Unfortunately, this works out to a cost of some $45 per visitor, a disaster by any advertising standard and one that will surely never be repeated.

What the dot.comers forgot, or never learned, is that building a brand requires consistency. They also ignored the importance of knowing exactly what their advertising was trying to achieve, and how to measure the outcome. Any money spent on advertising without clear results is money wasted.

Furthermore, branding takes a lot more than advertising. Branding results from many corporate actions, such as how you make your customers feel. If you make them feel bad, the finest advertising money can buy is worthless. Kevin O'Connor, chairman of Doubleclick, a Web advertising consultancy, has often told me that a consumer's defining experience with a brand is apt to occur not through hearing or seeing commercials, but in actual contact and experience. What a consumer thinks of an airline is usually based on his or her experience with that airline, not on the airline's advertising. In other words, advertising builds brand awareness, but that can be good or bad, depending on how you have treated the customer. Effective branding includes friendly customer service and honest communications. The Golden Rule never goes out of style.

Dollars alone don't build a brand. Because branding establishes the tone and terms for how a company presents itself publicly, it is essential that corporate and brand strategies be interwoven. Several fashion retailers do this exceptionally well. Abercrombie & Fitch, J. Crew, The Gap and The Gap's Old Navy, and Banana Republic are successful because, in addition to making huge investments in marketing, each store represents a very distinctive "look," which is consistent throughout that company regardless of the specific product. Someone can describe a friend who has an "Abercrombie & Fitch style"; everyone will conjure similar images associated with that brand and understand what it means. These retailers thoroughly integrate all aspects of the organization, that is, the marketing, advertising, and customer service.

Since the brand forms the company's "personality," it is crucial that all employees are in tune with both its tone and its specific message. There are two ways you can bring this about: over time, through osmosis, setting a corporate tone and hoping the employees will absorb it; or through intensive education, training, and incentives, which will be much quicker.

Either way, everyone in the organization must understand how big the stakes are. If the brand fails because employees lose track of its meaning and stop respecting its power, it will be impossible for the company to keep its promise to the consumer. It is a good bet that the company will also fail to reach its potential. Firestone, for instance, was hurt enormously when its tires were implicated in the rollover deaths of dozens of people riding in Ford Explorers. As I write, the jury is still out on whether Firestone's crisis is irreparable.

Johnson & Johnson, the health care products giant, survived a similar crisis in 1982 after someone smuggled cyanide into bottles of its Tylenol capsules on drugstore shelves, killing seven people. In a classic case of damage control, Johnson & Johnson instantly recalled 31 million bottles of Tylenol and redesigned its tamper-proof packaging, a response that cost $240 million but restored faith in Tylenol. In fact, Tylenol gained brand loyalty because the company faced the crisis with straight-shooting leadership.

Creating and establishing a brand is a complex and difficult process. It requires a little intuition and a lot of research and competitive analysis. The commercials we see on television are the result of what is often months of analysis and research, groping for the corporate personality and defining what the company will be. The target is clear: Your brand should evoke a unique image in the customer's mind, one so compelling that the customer automatically chooses your product from the scores of other possibilities in today's over-exposed world.

The importance of clarity in defining a brand was impressed on me during a talk I had in 1996 with Jan Horsfall at the time he became our vice president of marketing (before leaving us to run PhoneFree.com). He said he needed to understand the key words that our brand represented, the essence of our brand personality. He suggested some automotive analogies: "We aren't your quirky little VW Beetle, nor are we your luxury high-end sports car. We are a friendly family sedan that's safe, consistent, reliable, predictable, and used by the masses."

Up until this time, our efforts, as with so many other dot.coms, focused on how far out on the edge we could go. We naively thought we needed to be hip because we were an Internet company. In a few words, Jan had neatly summed up what we were and what we are. We were a Ford Taurus or a Toyota Corolla, because those are the cars people drive in mass. They are familiar and comfortable. Now, Jan said, we had to define and create the image in the minds of the public.

<GET RESULTS OR DON'T BOTHER>

Before Jan's arrival, our branding efforts resulted mainly in wasted spending. We bought some print advertisements, but applied them inconsistently; they could not have any effect, because we weren't sure what our objective was. We just had a feeling that we ought to be advertising, without understanding that ads are only the final step in the long, vital process of branding.

Advertising has to do more than announce a brand's value proposition. It has to deliver: The product has to live up to the advertising. It isn't hard to advertise and get people to try something once, but is very nearly impossible to bring them back after a disappointing experience. As my close friend Jack Connors, CEO of the advertising firm Hill Holiday has told me many times, "Nothing kills a bad product quicker than good advertising." A perfect example was the 1960s ad campaign in which the delightful cartoon characters Bert and Harry urged New Yorkers to try Piels beer. About a million did so. Their reaction proved only that Piels tasted awful, and the brand quickly died. "At the end of the day your brand is only as good as the product or service you sell," Tom Stemberg, founder of Staples, told me: "Nothing can ruin a good brand faster than a bad product."

The theme of the first Lycos campaign was "serendipity by design." We wanted to convey the idea that there is a whole new world on the Web just waiting to be explored, and that Lycos was positioned to make these serendipitous discoveries for you. It was a difficult theme to work with.

We built our print campaign around a creative concept that had "Lycos.com" showing up in a lot of unexpected places. For instance, in one ad, it was stamped on golf balls that were intended to evoke sperm cells floating through a field of blue. The ads got attention, and may have been "cool," but they didn't really say anything about us. We probably pushed away as many people as we drew.

Our inexperience showed most in our plan for the campaign climax: an ad showing "Lycos.com" carved out in a haircut on the back of a head that was supposed to evoke an image of Dennis Rodman, the notorious bad boy of basketball. This was when Rodman had Technicolor hair, paraded in a wedding dress and, in many people's eyes, in general, behaved outrageously. The hair-cut ad was to be the centerpiece of our campaign, which would coincide with the National Basketball Association playoffs.

When our attorneys saw the ad, they quickly scuttled it. If our objective was to have consumers think of Rodman, the attorneys said, we would have to pay for the right to use his image. If we didn't, Rodman would have the basis for a claim against us. We killed the piece, but the campaign was weak without it. In the end, we threw away a lot of money through inexperience and a lack of research.

Even if the Rodman ad had been as funny to readers as it was to us, it still would have been off target. In that ad, we were focusing on being cool, but we were not expressing the idea that using our product was how to become cool.

Before starting any ad campaign, you must thoroughly analyze every aspect of the strategy. This includes identifying the campaign's concept and its positioning. If you pay attention to detail, your campaign can have much broader effects than your budget would seem to indicate.

When Jan Horsfall came onboard, he hired a new agency, Bozell & Jacobs of New York, which turned into a very successful collaboration. They worked with Jan for several months to design a branding campaign. At that time, Lycos was still a search engine, rather than the multimedia-media, multiple-channel presence it has since become. But we already knew we wanted to be something more, and we knew that the whole image had to be wrapped up in our brand identity. But with all recognizing that I have a face made for radio, the idea quickly faded.

To our disadvantage, the name Lycos by itself means nothing to people, and it lacks the "personality" we felt was essential. We wanted Lycos to be much more identifiable. We talked about creating an icon around the name, with me or someone else as a brand personality, the way Virgin Air's founder and CEO Richard

Branson *is* Virgin, and the way Dave Thomas has become synonymous with Wendy's.

The agency's team then suggested the use of a dog to help create a personality behind the brand. Everyone loves dogs, they told us. First, they suggested a bloodhound that would find things no one else could by sniffing them out. We liked the bloodhound, but he was sad, droopy, and didn't capture the energy we were looking for. We wanted the Lycos brand to say "fast and easy." We wanted to convey the idea that Lycos instantly converts the Web's gigantic data library into highly useful information because our Web site is amazingly easy to access, understand, and navigate. The bloodhound somehow didn't conjure up the image of a speedster.

We next tried a beautiful black Labrador retriever as the Lycos dog, an idea that, according to our initial market research, consumers loved and understood immediately.

After extensive research, we were fairly confident that Lycos, the dog, would have the effect we sought, but we decided to hedge our bets by pairing the dog with a celebrity. At this point in Lycos' life, we could not afford the fees major celebrities commanded, but we found several who were willing to work for no pay in return for Lycos' promotion of their Web properties. I liked the idea of pairing Lycos with a beautiful woman, who would play to the starstruck national audience.

We settled on the model Claudia Schiffer. In the television spot we ran, someone shows Claudia's photograph to the dog who, whining in a happy, eager way, runs off; seconds later, her voice is heard—"Hi, I'm Claudia"—as the Lycos dog brings her back. It was very appealing.

The danger of using a celebrity in an ad campaign is that he or she can become too identified with your product. In this case, our audience research found that the dog was regarded as the star, as we intended, and Claudia was more of a character actor. People liked both players, the retriever and the retrieved.

We keep very detailed records of our page views. So we

were able to measure the ad's results immediately. The logs reflected a big overall spike in traffic right after the spots appeared. The campaign was an overnight success, and we had thousands more people visiting our site.

In short, the dog campaign was great creative advertising that worked. Over the next year, we saw our audience numbers continue to soar.

Branding 101

I can't emphasize enough that advertising campaigns are only the final stage of a lengthy branding process. Real branding can be achieved only with a thorough team effort. This effort must involve your employees, your customers, and your agency. The agency becomes as much a part of your corporate soul and fiber as any employee. It is essential that the agency understands your strategy and, in some cases, it may help to develop it. You need individuals with whom you can identify, work, and trust.

Both the company and the agency must first conduct extensive research on the brand and the competitive marketplace. Next, a positioning statement is developed that covers the general brand profile. This step may take several months and numerous revisions to get it right. The profile will identify how the company hopes to be perceived in the market. When a profile is done right, it is likely to be around for a long time.

When complete, you must set the strategic goal of the campaign, which will vary widely depending on your product. General Motors, for example, doesn't have to persuade people that cars are convenient, just why its products should be preferred over other brands. Internet companies, on the other hand, often must show what the Web can do for people before touting its specific products. Only when the profile and strategic goals are clear does the work on the actual advertisements begin.

A creative team from the agency, along with key people from the company, produce concepts and storyboards. Rarely does the right campaign emerge immediately. More often, the team will develop many approaches, some of which you will build on, others, you will throw away, until the team arrives at a campaign that everyone feels comfortable with.

I was involved in every step of our branding process, as any chief executive must be when the issue at hand is nothing less than defining the personality of the company. This is not to say that you need to look at every step along every road. But defining the company's persona is a top priority of any successful leader. Though I made my share of mistakes, I grew more experienced and learned to trust my intuition regarding how to best convey to our customers what the essence of Lycos was.

Once you have worked out the concept of the campaign the next step is to deal with media placement. This means determining where, when, and how often you intend to run the campaign, decisions that will shape the actual ads. Among the alternatives are national television, spot television in local markets, national cable, selected programming, all print, some combination of newspapers and/or magazines, outdoor, radio, and pop-up. (The pop-up technique puts ads in unexpected venues as a way of adding an element of surprise to the campaign.) Or any combination of the above.

Media placement is every bit as important as the creative work, and it is easy to make mistakes. If you are starting a new sports magazine, for instance, you might advertise heavily on televised sports broadcasts, until you realize that you have targeted people who only watch television and won't buy your magazine.

In our case, we decided to focus primarily on reaching a national audience through national cable television, and would aim in part at the "water cooler" audience. That meant placing our commercials on programs that people talk about around the water cooler the next day: "Did you see *ER*?" A good media strategist can capture public attention completely out of proportion to the dollars you spend.

You have to be smart and work hard to build a brand; sometimes the smart moves aren't the most obvious ones. Somewhere around early 1996, some of our competitors began to advertise on television, and I wondered why a Web brand would waste money on television. A short time later, I was attempting to recruit a marketing executive into the company who went on to become the president of Dunkin' Donuts. He answered that question for me quite succinctly, explaining that "a point of market share will never be as cheap for an Internet company as it is today." He was right. At that point, no competitor had differentiated itself, and the big audience was yet to come online; then, if ever, was the time to establish a brand.

TV advertising was actually a brilliant tactic for newly created companies on the Internet. In 1995 and 1996, it was very cost-effective to deliver your message because the market wasn't yet crowded. Though we missed the early opportunity, it was not too late. When we started the dog campaign, it was still possible to break through with a Web brand on television for a relative bargain. Today, although it remains every bit as feasible, it would be a lot more expensive and an enormous effort. The field has become very crowded.

Once committed to a campaign, testing becomes the next step. When you are devoting millions of dollars to the effort, it is vital that you assess its efficacy immediately. If it is not working, you can make changes right away. At Lycos, we paraded people, one at a time, past the storyboards and tried to gauge their initial reactions.

After deciding on the dog-named-Lycos approach, we used focus groups and our instincts to fine-tune the specifics of the television spot. In the early commercials, we created an unnatural color scheme by intensifying nature's colors; for example, the sky was a brighter blue and the grass a brighter green. The effect was a sort of fantastic realism; like a cartoon and, simultaneously, real. We also developed the tag line for the ad, "Go get it." On one level, it simply meant that Lycos the dog could find whatever you sought quickly and easily. On another level, we were telling viewers that Lycos the Web site would also obey orders to go find whatever they needed. The public seemed to understand that, and our audience flourished.

The second version of our ad campaign was tailored to

reflect the company's new dimensions. Jan Horsfall had left to start his own company. A new agency, Hill Holiday, focused the next wave of commercials on the areas of content available on Lycos—games, music, e-mail, finance, shopping, and many other properties that now comprise Lycos.com. It was an evolution of the original compaign, reflecting a very important point in brand development. Companies evolve, and brands must evolve with them.

The basics of advertising

Television advertising should never be your only marketing effort. When building a brand, it is useful to leverage your promotional dollars with unconventional tactics. Just a few of these include pop-ups, viral marketing, guerrilla marketing, and public relations.

POP-UPS. As I noted earlier, these are advertising or promotional materials that "pop up" in unexpected places. As Jeff Bezos, of Amazon.com, likes to say, "In sight, in mind."

The premise of pop-ups is that the ad's effect is reinforced by the element of surprise that results because the public doesn't associate your brand with the new environment. In 1997, for example, we sponsored a race car on the NASCAR circuit, which no Web company had done before. This was an opportunity not only because NASCAR is the most heavily attended spectator sport in the United States, but because the demographics of its audience align almost perfectly with those of the typical Web user.

Initially, people were surprised and intrigued when we sponsored a race called the Lycos.com 250. When our own car won the race, we trucked the car around the country for appearances, and the driver chatted online once a week. Eventually, viewers watched for our car each week to see how it performed. A toy company even sold Lycos toy cars in stores across the country.

We continue to use pop-ups. At major sporting events—the

World Series, the Super Bowl, the Ryder Cup, the U.S. Open, Wimbledon—we hire planes to skywrite the "Lycos" name or fly a Lycos banner. TV cameras often pick up the banner at these high-end sporting events, which attract the most influential of spectators—CEOs, marketing executives, people with considerable power to buy advertising. These are key moments for show-the-flag stunts that help grow the brand in the minds of people we need on our side. At this level, the strategy is more for less. Again, consider: At last year's Super Bowl, just one 30-second TV spot cost $2.2 million. For only $2,500 per game, we hired planes to fly above the football venues, hauling a huge Lycos banner that was seen from both seats at the game or from a quick shot of our plane on TV screens. This surely did not provide the power of a full 30-second advertisement, but such an approach saves a lot of money when you just cannot or should not be spending more. Effective advertising does not have to be expensive adverstising.

VIRAL MARKETING. This is marketing used often on the Internet, whereby users beget other users at geometric speed. Viral marketing has been a powerful and important tactic. In our case, we couldn't afford to spend much on promotion, so we looked for properties whose very business models ensured that they would be marketed by word of mouth.

For example, Tripod, one of our early purchases, offers visitors the chance to create their own Web pages. People who build personal Web pages usually do so because they are proud of what they have done, and want to tell other people about themselves, their families, hobbies, jobs, or just about anything else. They create their site, then tell their friends and family to visit the page. That leads to more new customers, who go on to spread the word to still more people.

To date, about 25 million people have built personal homepages through our services without a dollar spent promoting the sites. This is 100 percent viral marketing: It builds upon, develops, and supports itself.

Viral marketing can be applied to any product; you have to develop a plan, think creatively, integrate it with your strategic goals, and involve consumers in something that will spread without any further effort on your part.

GUERRILLA MARKETING. Another tactic that lets us do more with less, guerrilla marketing involves enticing and persuading your partners, employees, and others to promote your brand on their own and without remuneration.

In your employee gatherings, for instance, you might focus on how one employee can make a difference and that every employee can be a brand evangelist.

I used to tell employees they should feel an obligation to find new Lycos customers. If they are proud of the company, and proud of the service that we provide, this should come naturally to them. After all, we were a leading-edge company in a very exciting medium. Certainly, I thought our products were the best in the business, and I wanted them to think so as well. I asked them to choose one Lycos product that they thought two of their friends or relatives would like and get them to try it; after that, try two more products and two more friends, and so on. It's a great way to generate excitement for your products from the ground up.

We gave packages of bumper stickers to employees when they joined the company, and hoped they would plaster them all over town. Some people, of course, did it to excess. When we took a few hundred people to a baseball game at Fenway Park for one of our employee nights, people slapped hundreds of them on anything that didn't move. We kept a red wagon full of Lycos bumper stickers in the reception area of our headquarters; visitors were encouraged to take as many as they like.

After sponsoring the NASCAR racer, we offered employees the chance to have their own cars painted like the Lycos race car. With some luck, we thought, maybe, someone would volunteer. To our astonishment, 67 employees, some of whom had brand-new vehicles, agreed to have them painted, decals and all. The cars became permanent moving commercials for Lycos. These are examples of guerilla tactics, which, when they work, are extremely effective and cost next to nothing.

Another idea we had was to make costumes of Lycos the dog available for people to take to beaches, parades, and other public events. The employees volunteered, on their own time, to dress up as the Lycos dog and hand out key chains, bumper stickers, diskettes and the like. Believe it or not, there was a waiting list for the costumes.

We worked hard to create an environment in which people were truly proud that they worked at Lycos. Not everyone, no matter what line of work, would put a corporate bumper sticker on his or her car, let alone have the car painted like a billboard. If your company shares this kind of loyalty, make use of it. For example, one of our workers was a parachutist, and his chute carried our logo. Some employees had Lycos logos on their snowboards or even in their swimming pools. The employee evangelist worked so well that we even had some who tatooed the company logo on their bodies. It is one thing to have a product that people like; it is yet another to have a brand that evokes passion so stong that people will paint their cars or their bodies with it. When our people sang the praises of the company, they sang hallelujah from the highest mountaintop.

PUBLIC RELATIONS. PR is essential, usually free, and often more effective than its costly cousin—advertising. Its guidelines are straightforward: Build and maintain a strong relationship with the media. Get to know a good reporter at a key news outlet, and meet with him or her periodically, even when you don't have news. Help them understand the state of your business and your strategy. That way, when you do have news or hit a crisis, your contact will have the background for writing the piece you would prefer to the one you might get otherwise.

Two insights will save you much grief with reporters. First, the news business is intensely competitive. A valid scoop that beats the competition is the holy grail of reporting. The more you can help provide it, the more likely your side of the story will be told fairly and fully. Second, reporters spend their lives cultivating sources of information the public doesn't yet know. Reliable sources are essential to gain access, generate scoops, and verify information. Make yourself a reliable source and you will help some reporter get their job done. Needless to say, your own private interests and public relations will not suffer. The media should be looked at as your friends. A group of professionals doing their job with or without your cooperation.

Given their competitiveness, news media leap at anything big, hot, dramatic, and first. They have no interest in your story, however cosmic, if they see it as dull, minor, or yesterday's news. Accordingly, be selective about what you announce. Face the fact that the 950th partnership you just signed is non-news in the eyes of the guardians of the news. By using news releases sparingly and judiciously, you're far more likely to get the attention you deserve when you have something really important to say.

When pitching a story to the media, package the idea as a complete story. For example, don't pretend you have no competitors—suggest they be included. The more complete the story idea, the more likely the reporter will write it.

Master the key elements of news. They include newness, conflict, surprise, human interest, entertainment, usefulness, and relevance to a particular news market's particular audience. Is the story telling people something they didn't know, need to know, and will be amazed, amused, delighted, saddened, or uplifted to know? Will this story make us believers or disbelievers? In sum, is it worth a busy reader's time? Yes, if it's a man-bites-dog surprise. No, if it's the opposite. As one veteran editor used to tell his writers, "Make me laugh or cry, but make me feel."

Some PR do's and don'ts:

- Do prepare for every interview. Determine what your major messages are beforehand and limit them to no more than three. Anticipate the hardest questions you may be asked. Prepare for the worst and hope for the best.

- Do make sure your answers are truthful, concise, memorable, jargon-free—and on message.
- Do understand that reporters are paid skeptics who suspect you're not telling the whole truth (but hope you are); that they detest being used for blatant commercial purposes as well as being blamed for grilling you (their job); that nothing pleases them more than a good quote and nothing will keep your interview out of print faster (if that's what you want) than your being totally unquotable.
- Do answer only the questions you want to answer in the way you want to answer—and stay on message.
- Don't burn bridges. Reporters tend to be reporters for life and are likely to move around. Maintain good relationships; you'll have good results.
- Don't use "No comment" unless you're legally bound to do so, as under court orders. Evasion convinces press and public that you're trying to hide something.
- Don't pay for news coverage, whether in cash or in promising to buy an ad in exchange for a future story. Paying the press (to say nothing of the press accepting or soliciting payment) is akin to bribery and will inevitably come back to bite you.
- Don't ever hold a press conference unless you have something truly big to say. Reporters resent having their time wasted and will hold it against you next time.
- Don't assume that something you tell a reporter is off the record, unless you insist that it is and make sure he or she understands that. The reporter's job is to get news out of you, the more controversial the news, the better. As the *Washington Post*'s Bob Woodward once warned, "Everything is off the record unless it's really good."

Our brand is our destiny

The process of building and sustaining a brand should be approached with care, thought, hard work, and a lot of help from your friends. It is your strength, your identity, and your destiny. In the world's eyes, we are what others think we are, and for companies, as for individuals, hardly anything is more important than acquiring well-deserved approval. Great brands, like great reputations, are better earned with deeds than bought with dollars, but in either case they are priceless and irreplaceable. "Who steals my purse steals trash," Shakespeare wrote. "But he that filches from me my good name ... makes me poor indeed." A good brand not only creates wealth. It is your company's very life. Don't let anybody filch it.

Profit is not a four-letter word

6

SOME TRUTHS PASS THE TEST OF TIME. With few exceptions, the fundamental rules of business fall into this category. Though there may be long, dizzying periods when they seem irrelevant, but sooner or later the basics win out. For example, could anyone dispute Warren Buffett when he says: "Rule number one: Never lose money. Rule number two: Never forget rule number one."

Although occasionally criticized for missing one of the strongest bull markets in history, Buffett was steadfast in his belief that there would be a significant consolidation of technology and Internet companies—and a corresponding correction in their stock prices. It was two years ago that I first heard him express this view. With great wit and a lifetime of experience, he compared—with strong statistical support—the plethora of Internet stocks with the abundance of automotive companies in the early twentieth century. He predicted that the simple laws of supply and demand all but guaranteed a pull back. "Ultimately," he said, "those that make money will survive."

In the spring of 2000, the markets got a major reality check—after nearly three years during which illusion ruled. During that heady, almost surreal, period investors were driven by what U.S. Federal Reserve Chairman Alan Greenspan famously called "irrational exuberance." The markets valued high-tech start-ups regardless of their (often nonexistent) profits, and relied instead on multiples of revenues, the more cosmic the better. Wishful thinking ruled.

In the history of the U.S. stock market, there are few parallels for the recent frenzy. We have to look back 70 years—to the 1929 crash, which was also preceded by an enormous stock run-up—to find a comparison.

What's remarkable—and confirms that segments of the market were in a "bubble"—is the fact that there were no analogous spikes in other economic indicators. For example, as the market was reaching its unprecedented highs—the Dow Jones Industrial Average stood at about 3,600 in early 1994 and exceeded 11,000 by 1999—personal income and gross domestic product grew less than 30 percent, half of which can be attributed to inflation. During the same period, corporate profits increased less than 60 percent, and the average price of a single-family home was up just 9 percent. If we juxtapose these figures with a 200-percent upsurge in stock market values, it's not surprising that the bubble burst.

Although the United States enjoyed truly meteoric stock market growth between 1994 and 1999, the valuations in France, Germany, Italy, Spain, and the United Kingdom doubled, while Canada's nearly doubled, and Australia's grew by half. Then reality hit with a vengeance.

The stock prices of companies that had never made a profit fell en masse more than 95 percent. Equally telling, a company as legendary as AT&T—which generates enormous profits—was under so much pressure from its poor revenue growth that in October 2000, it gave up its goal of dominating the telecommunications industry and announced plans to split into four separate companies. As it always does in the long run, the market rewards simultaneous growth and profits, not one at the expense of the other.

Now that we've had time to take a deep breath and analyze the plunging markets, two points are clear. The first lesson, which seems to be one we need to learn over and over, is that securities markets can be misleading. In recent years, one school of economists has argued that markets are "efficient"—that is, they take into account all available information and thus accurately reflect economic reality. Yet, very little in the real world gyrates as wildly as the NASDAQ average. In my view, the markets reflect a temporary consensus—subject to misperceptions, hype, fear, and sudden change. There's also a strong element of imagination, emotion, and greed at play.

The second lesson is that, in the long run, the stock market's winners are companies with something the bubble-boomers never acquired—a compelling vision backed up by a solid infrastructure capable of delivering on that vision. Only that combination is capable of generating not only consistent revenue growth, but profitability, too.

Economist Dick Sabot echoes the view that the companies that will thrive into the twenty-first century are "those that have their feet squarely on the ground and can demonstrate a profitable business model." He views the market's current position, he told me, as "the second phase of the Internet revolution" in which "the emphasis has shifted from growth to profitability ... a healthy shift."

Likewise, Don Keough, former President of The Coca-Cola Company and chairman of Allen & Company, believes that an obvious tenet bears repetition, as he explained in a recent conversation: "Whether you talk old economy or new economy, the only reason people invest in a corporation is to earn a fair return on their investment. In the early days of the technology explosion, people were pouring money into stocks instead of into companies." In other words, many investors became dazzled by promise, not profit. Surely no one who took the time to carefully research an Internet start-up with no profits and no proven delivery model would have invested. Basically there would be little more than a name and a clever-sounding idea. Yet tens of thousands of investors did just that.

At the risk of joining the I-told-you-so chorus, I admit that I always thought the bloated valuations couldn't last. Perhaps it's the influence of my New England upbringing, and seeing my parents' struggle to pay the mortgage, but I've always tended toward fiscal conservatism.

In the days before the markets rediscovered rational exuberance, investors treated Lycos well enough, but my frugality wasn't universally popular. I remember being chided by one influential Wall Street analyst for being too profit-oriented—an attitude I didn't understand and actually found shocking.

Lycos never joined the stampede for growth at any cost, and from the beginning we aimed to be profitable. To some extent, we had no choice. Unlike so many other web start-ups, we weren't showered with venture money. Venture capital comes with a lot of strings attached—not the least of which is the dilution of equity. Further, as a public company we had presented an earnings-based financial model that we were expected to follow. We were proud to stand by that model and proud of the reputation for consistency that we developed. In fact, for the 19 consecutive quarters I was at the helm, we met or exceeded Wall Street's expectations. Meeting these numbers wasn't an option— it was an obligation. The one time we came close to missing our earnings forecast, we nearly turned the company inside out to recover.

It came during a period when we were aggressively buying companies and hiring employees; during that particular quarter we had hired close to 200 people, boosting total staffing by nearly 30 percent. And we were advertising heavily. One day early in the fourth quarter of 1999, Ted Philip, Lycos' CFO, came into my office, ashen, and said that we weren't going to meet our projections. "The only way we're going to avoid this," he said, "is to be bold, tough, and Draconian. Are we up for it?"

We were. Had we missed the forecast, the valuation of the company would be cut in half overnight and our credibility would be shot. Slamming the brakes on our fast-moving freight train, we stopped all advertising, eliminated all outside contractors, and cut every unnecessary expense we could find. We didn't fill new positions or replace people who left the company.

We also worked hard to make sure everyone understood the urgency of the crisis. We wanted every employee to pitch in. In a company-wide meeting, I explained what was happening and showed them, among other things, comparable numbers at Yahoo! If they could succeed, so could we. I visited all of our locations, pointing out how carelessly we'd all been spending. Requests had already been submitted to hire another 200 or 300 employees. There were also requests to spend tens of millions for computer systems and marketing. I explained to our staff that we were no different than a household: what goes out can't exceed what comes in. In the long run, it's the only way we could keep our jobs. Everyone rallied to the cause and in the end we beat the estimates.

Markets are pretty simple—over time they demand growth in both sales and profits. A company can lose money, sometimes for extended periods, but it had better have either the vision or the capital to carry its bottom line back into the black. Lycos was a profitable company as far back as October 1997. This was quite a rarity. Even today, you could probably count the number of profitable Internet companies on two hands.

One of the very few companies that beat us in the earnings race was our archrival, Yahoo! Showing their first profits in late 1996, the company quickly demonstrated remarkable earnings power, producing operating margins in the 40 percent range. For all the criticism the industry is taking, we should note that there are very few companies in the world capable of generating those figures. At one point the company's market valuation topped $130 billion dollars: It had become one of the most highly valued companies in the world based on its ability to grow both the top and bottom lines.

Markets, however, can be as punishing as they are rewarding. The slightest hint of a slowdown triggers a chain reaction.

This was one of the problems on the NASDAQ in 2000. Markets became skittish over an early wave of dot.com failures. Public and private financing tightened. This cause and effect meant there were fewer companies spending on advertising and infrastructure. This, of course, led to slowing growth for companies that provide those products and services. The self-fulfilling prophecy then complete, valuations tumbled, even for companies that had yet to stumble. Yahoo!, like Mark Twain, claimed that rumors of its demise were greatly exaggerated. Quarter after quarter, there were whispers that the company would miss its expectations, but quarter after quarter it performed. Despite its success, the fear gripping the markets caused Yahoo! to lose almost $120 billion of its value. Even with that staggering loss, it remained one of the most highly valued Internet stocks. As well it should—the company has proven itself.

The rules don't change. Lose sight of the bottom line and look out below. Financial markets require growth and they require profits. Provide both, and the possibilities are endless.

To be sure, it is all tightly intertwined. The quickest path to bottom-line growth, for instance, is revenue growth. A company needs a relentless focus on increasing sales, expanding markets, and developing new customers.

A key rule for earnings growth is to thoroughly understand your market. Pinpoint exactly where you can best succeed—that is, what market can your company own? Start with Jack Welch's famous directive to General Electric: "If you can't be number one or number two in your category get out of the business." Then add: Reinvent that category or invent a new one that you can lead.

Welch's strategy—which he implemented when he first came to GE in the early 1980s—translated into $10 billion worth of divestitures, the cutting of more than 120,000 jobs in the remaining businesses, and $17 billion in acquisitions. The point is that companies need to assess their portfolios and cut loose any businesses that can't or don't succeed.

It's not my intention that this book be a guide for growing revenues. That's a topic unto itself. Suffice it to say that an organization needs an ethos of hard work and commitment—and it needs an ethos that understands the necessity of sales. All too often I've heard the lament that a company is being distracted by its customers. This is a cancerous and deadly viewpoint. Within the common sense boundaries of remaining consistent with a vision and strategy, every company needs to be sales focused.

A few years back a group at Lycos decided that their job was to protect the user from an onslaught of advertising. Their content, they declared, would remain advertising-free. This ludicrous concept was short-lived to say the least. Yes, our end users were our primary customers. But to suggest we shouldn't profit from them just lacked common sense. It would be analogous to Procter & Gamble developing a shampoo, designing a gorgeous display rack, and then prohibiting sales less the beauty of the display be disrupted.

It's not hard to understand that more sales are the key to profit. Of course, cost control is also important, but no company ever cost-contained itself to greatness. The bottom line in my message is to be sure that you grow the top line.

On the Internet, there are as many different types of revenue streams as there are business. I'll touch on three of the most significant.

The first is providing infrastructure—servers, computers, high-speed lines, security, hosting, software, etc. This is what Cisco, Exodus, Compaq, Oracle, and others do very successfully. These companies provide the backbone upon which the consumer experience is built.

The second source is e-commerce: selling goods and services. This can include business-to-consumer (Amazon.com), business-to-business (Cisco.com), or even consumer-to-consumer (eBay.com). The sheer size of the markets is astounding: over $28 billion in sales in 2000, expected to reach $86 billion by 2003.

The third source of revenue is where Lycos made its mark—

advertising. Advertising is a $270 billion market in the United States alone. The Web nabbed over $8 billion of that in 2000, up 74 percent from 1999. It's a very basic concept. Develop a customer base—then find companies willing to pay to reach that audience. On the Web, relatively few companies have developed an audience that is large and consistent enough to attract advertisers to a platform where fees range from $1 to $200 CPM's. (CPM is the industry term for cost per thousand and means that at a $100 CPM, for instance, you would pay $100,000 for one million viewings of an ad.) The fee is determined by variables that range from supply and demand to the degree of consumer targeting a site can deliver.

As I mentioned though, few companies can prosper in the online advertising market. In January of 2000, Lycos was generating over 350 million page views per day (a page view is a unit of measure in online advertising—each represents a content screen viewed by a user). An unbelievable number when you consider it was zero in 1995.

The need to compete with numbers like that makes it very difficult for new sites to break into the market. In addition, the technology has become increasingly complex and advertisers' demand for scale has soared. Coca-Cola isn't interested in buying tiny packages of advertising; it demands a concentrated ad purchase that reaches millions of consumers at a time. This traps small sites in a Catch 22: They can't attract advertisers because they don't have the audience, they can't invest in marketing to get the audience because they don't have the revenue, and they can't build page views because they're not marketing, and so on.

In contrast, established companies reap benefits everywhere they turn. As computer chips get faster and cheaper, prices of personal computers go down and more people buy them. As more users go online, the infrastructure companies invest more heavily. As a result, connection speeds improve and more people want to go online. Before you know it, your family has two or three PCs, and you're managing your finances, friendships, and photo albums on the Internet.

The more those consumers log on, the more the large media companies can invest in content. As content gets stronger, it attracts more consumers, which means greater revenues from advertisers. Again, we see the domino effect, this time to the company's benefit.

Building an online audience is deceptively easy. If you spend enough money, you can entice a viewer to take a look. The question is whether or not you can hold on to that viewer. Does your service, product, or content offer a value proposition? Does the consumer return not only once, but time after time? Does it build enough scale to attract advertisers and cover your inevitable losses during the startup period? Finally, is it organic—does your very presence in the marketplace attract more consumers?

There may be a total of 20 to 25 companies that are now capable of building a successful online media franchise. And the reason they're able to do so comes right back to the theme of this chapter: They generate profits. It's not an 80:20 rule. It's more like a 99:1 rule. The Web comprises more than 1 billion sites. Simple arithmetic reveals that at least 999,999,975 of them must either find another source of revenue, or live on as sidelines for the leaders.

If I make only one point in this book, I hope it's my belief in the profit principle. It requires discipline and focus. Looking so far ahead that you ignore today's demands, and spending beyond your means are both sure paths to disaster. Yet companies do it every day.

Dan Nova told me that he believes that in the frenzied late 1990s we were experiencing a cycle in which "too much money was spent too quickly. Companies that develop too quickly and put their costs and expenses too far in front of the revenue curve run the risk of running out of money, which, in an uncertain financing environment, is potentially disastrous for a young company. What we see now, as a result, is that many companies aren't being financed and many companies are running out of money because they spent too much early on in the development cycle." You only have to read the business pages to confirm Dan's words. It seems that almost every day there's a story about another once-high-flying dot.com that has crashed and burned. A lot of employees are losing their jobs and a lot of investors are losing their shirts.

At Lycos, we moved quickly but with great deliberation. The conviction that we could build a better financial model was the deciding factor in many of our early acquisitions. It was surely the case with Tripod. The company was profitless, but promising. But even our belief that we could turn it around quickly didn't prevent us from agonizing over the market's reaction to the deal. Lycos was now a moneymaker; how would investors view our swallowing a money loser? We pledged a quick return to profitability, went ahead with the deal—and the market applauded.

We acquired more than a dozen companies in all. Each had been floundering, but they all had exceptional brands and consumer loyalty. By making them part of the Lycos network, we were able to leverage those assets.

Quote.com, for example, was an excellent site for financial services but it was losing a lot of cash. We had already passed up the opportunity once to buy it for that reason, but in September 1999 we told its managers that we'd be interested if they would cut costs, including major staff reductions. They did. We closed the deal on a Tuesday and by Wednesday Quote.com was operating as a profitable business with less than half of its original payroll. Employee morale soared in the streamlined company, which became one of our better revenue producers. We used the same model with Gamesville, Matchmaker.com, and several others.

The essential point is that we ran our acquisitions as brands, not as companies, and we demanded a sound return on investment from our brand managers. This allowed us to concentrate on audience growth while simultaneously lowering costs. We centralized accounting, human resources, management information, and we consolidated sales and management information systems. The one thing we always kept intact was the audience, the customer base. It follows the first and last rule of any acquisition: keep the customers and keep the revenue streams flowing.

In many ways, my message belies the stereotypical image of a freewheeling Internet start-up. Many people think of Web companies as collections of creative geniuses in cut-offs and T-shirts, working in offices with zany, irreverent graffiti on the walls. But in the end the business of the Internet is business, and the business of business is profits.

More than anything else, profitability requires a relentless determination to balance the budget. It's essential to forecast demand as precisely as possible, and not bloat an organization with people and processes. Develop a culture that's passionate about earnings; establish strict financial controls to ensure smart spending; institute an information system that monitors and reports the company's total spending *every day*. Maintaining financial control requires fierce diligence. After all, as Melissa Bradley, founder and president, BHC Inc., points out, "Control doesn't come with the title of CEO; control comes with the cash."

What follows are a few of the rules I always followed to ensure our company was fiscally disciplined and focused on profitability. Some might be obvious, but, collectively, they will likely add to any company's bottom line.

1. Responsibility includes empowerment

Managers should be fully in charge of their departments' spending. When confronted with unforeseen expenses, I don't want them asking me, "How should I pay for this?" I want them telling me how they paid for it and what the return will be.

2. Responsibility includes accountability

Managers should succeed or fail, in part, based on their fiscal management. Budget both from the top down, based on the revenue plan, and from the bottom up, with each department proposing what it can deliver and what it will cost. Reconcile the two views to get realistic figures. For managers, fiscal honesty should be the only option. You want to create a check and balance within a group to prevent runaway enthusiasm and unrealistic promises.

3. Fiscal goals must always be aligned with strategic goals

Compensation plans need to be directly tied to corporate, strategic, and financial goals. At Lycos, we also made sure that all employees understood our financial goals: There were periodic updates on the company's progress and—every quarter or so—we offered all employees the same road-show presentation that we gave to investors. I made a point of comparing every line on our income statement with those of competitors, so that everyone understood what we were up against and how we were faring.

All of this underlined my view that the company budget is an investment tool, not a checkbook. It helped our employees at Lycos understand that spending had a collective purpose in which they all played a role.

4. Every employee must feel like a stakeholder in the company

I felt it was essential that we issue stock options to each employee—at the end of 2000, more than 200 employees were "Lycos millionaires." When someone made a budget request, I often asked, "If this were your own money, would you still spend it?" The answers I got indicated that the "if" was irrelevant; people felt it *was* their money.

5. It's essential to have strong internal controls that make it impossible for anyone to act with impropriety

A vice president of finance, for instance, might be the only one who can wire funds, but before he can do so the bank must call an authorized company representative to verify the transaction. This isn't creating a police state, it's being true to your fiduciary obligations and safeguarding your firm's assets.

If your financial controls are strict, it's not because you don't trust your employees. It's because a tight process works to alert the company before money is spent. There is an obvious element of monitoring as well, and I view that positively. To not have a system of checks and balances is careless.

6. You must have firm, clear rules to which everyone adheres without exception

At Lycos, invoices without a purchase order would not be paid. One manager learned that the hard way: He had to pay a $2,000 bill for a conference facility out of his own pocket because he'd failed to get a purchase order. That was painful, but it was a violation of the policy, and we had to prove that we stood behind that policy.

7. Anticipate demand and have clear plans to accommodate it

How many people do you expect to buy your goods in the next quarter, and how will you meet that demand? Don't make the mistake Sony did during the Christmas season of 2000, when its PlayStation2 could have been a runaway success had the company's manufacturing and distribution systems been prepared. Since they weren't, enormous demand went unmet.

Profits have always been my first and last measurement. And the few times I've lost sight of that, were the times I almost made serious mistakes. Probably the most memorable of those near misses was a merger, we came close to making with NBC.

Late 1998 was a time when much of traditional media felt an urgent need to expand its online presence. Internet audience growth was soaring, and industry analysts were speculating that the Web was drawing viewers away from other mediums, such as television.

At face value, the concept of an alliance with a television network was inviting (this was before any proposed merger with USA). Disney had already teamed with our Silicon Valley rival, Infoseek and rumors of other deals were rampant. The prospect of a relationship with NBC was appealing. The network had a reputation for excellence, was the most aggressive of the big four broadcasters on the Web having already forged an alliance with CNET in the launching of a portal named Snap and its ownership by General Electric gave it great marquee value.

Our companies had intense dialogue for several weeks. NBC's negotiation team, was led by Tom Rogers, executive vice president and now CEO at magazine publisher Primedia. Tom and all the GE and NBC representatives impressed me as people of determination and impeccable character. Rogers was on a mission to replicate on the Web the great success the network had enjoyed in expanding into cable with properties such as CNBC and MSNBC. As time passed, we gained momentum under a deal structure that called for NBC to contribute many of its Web assets to Lycos. Further, Lycos would have traded between $250 and $300 million in equity for an equivalent amount of television promotion on the network. In return, NBC would have owned about one third of the new company.

Throughout the process, I was caught between the lure of a big network and what would have become a very distressed income statement should we merge. Ted Philip reminded me of this nearly every hour of every day as he cautioned that such a merger would destroy any hope of earnings for years to come. The source of the profit problem was two-fold: first, the equity to be traded for advertising would have to be reflected as expense for the company. We would be picking more than $50 million per year in additional expense from this alone. Second, all of the Web sites being contributed by NBC, such as nbc.com, were young businesses throwing off their own losses that we would need to absorb.

We spent countless hours attempting to bridge this gap. We asked NBC to contribute cash or stock instead of promotion. We asked them to subsidize the losses of the Web subsidiaries. It was not to happen. NBC, and ultimately GE, was not willing to offer its stock for the stock of a new company. It became clear that this deal was making less and less sense for Lycos shareholders. If GE was concerned enough about the value proposition that it was not going to buy in with cold, hard cash—how could we justify building a shaky financial model just for the sake of having a glamorous new partner. True, in 1998 the market's euphoria may have applauded the deal, but I am not so sure they would still be applauding in 2001.

There is no doubt that NBC would have been a great partner. Both Jack Welch and NBC's president, Bob Wright, worked through various stages of the deal in an attempt to create a mutually satisfying structure. In the end we could not find it.

Coming at it from two entirely different perspectives, this deal may have been doomed from the start. The NBC/GE teams understandably shied away from any adverse impact to their P&L, or, for that matter, any type of dilutive framework. Their goal was to own our platform while offloading any losses they were accumulating. Similarly, our goal was to capture the benefit of their promotion and advertising without needing to reflect this expense on our own income statement. Our commitment to earnings was shared, but the bits and pieces we would be trading to structure a deal meant one company would have to sacrifice the bottom line. Neither was willing to do so. Two companies focused the most basic of business mandates—earnings—resulted in a deal that just could not happen.

The ultimate prize for a successful corporation is its ability to offer shareholders a return. That return is profits. Keeping your sights on that same place is sound advice for any businessperson.

Be great

at what you're good at

7

IN DECEMBER OF 2000, I became involved in a public-service campaign to attract new recruits for the U.S. Air Force. In conjunction with the campaign, I agreed to fly on a T-38 Talon supersonic jet out of Randolph Air Force Base in Texas, piloted by Lieutenant Colonel Murray "Mur Dog" Roberts. I experienced some of the most amazing aerobatics one could imagine as this powerful jet rolled, inverted, and dove, pulling over 6.5 Gs. Even more impressive than the power of the aircraft was the competence of the men and women of the Air Force Educational and Training Command (AETC). The Command is responsible for all aspects of flight training and support across the globe and operates in an environment where the margin of error is literally a matter of life and death.

As complex as any large corporation, with over 40,000 employees, advanced technology, and a mission to protect national security and freedom, the AETC has helped build the world's strongest air force by being great at what it is good at. Its discipline of the highest order and personnel specialization in every detail made me think that business could learn much from our military's successes.

Despite criticism against them, the United States armed services long ago achieved the status that most corporations ceaselessly strive toward—they are number one in the world. They have done it with a keen understanding and a laser-beam focus upon their core competencies. Each unit within each command, within each branch of the military, has a specific mission at which it becomes expert. The Air Force, for instance, does not assign pilots to maintenance crews, nor does the Navy expect its sailors to participate in land battles. Each group strives to be great, not good, in its area. Businesses need to do the same.

To paraphrase Vince Lombardi, greatness isn't everything in business; it is the only thing. The quickest path to disaster for all but a few of today's multinational corporations is to become a jack of all trades and master of none. Instead, we should aspire to become a master of few.

Business is so competitive today that being good is simply not good enough. We live in a winner-take-all marketplace. Nearly every field is dominated by a very small number of companies.

Although competition, technology, and even the ways in which business is transacted have changed enormously, one thing has not—nothing short of excellence will suffice. *NBC Nightly News* anchor Tom Brokaw was quoted describing how he learned that lesson. "My first job was mowing lawns. I had a push mower, and I said to my father, 'I could make a lot more money with a power mower.' My dad was a Mr. Fix-It type, so he went into the garage and built me one—out of a little old motor, some black plywood, and a few pipes. I was embarrassed when I saw it. I thought, I can't be pushing that around. All of my friends are going to have slick-looking machines. Kids did tease me at first—until they realized that my mower could go through anything. So I got the toughest jobs in town, and suddenly I was making more money than I could count. The experience was a real lesson for me. It showed me that what counts above all is the excellence of your work."

If it appears that Brokaw's first job has little in common with his current position, I would suggest otherwise. He has been successful at both for identical reasons: Then, as now, he had access to the necessary technology, he was unafraid to undertake the "toughest jobs in town," he remained determined to perform the job flawlessly, and he learned to confront public scorn.

The National Football League is another example of a business that owns a market because, in the narrow area in which it concentrates, it is great. Though several other leagues have tried, none have been able to reproduce the entertaining sports experience that the NFL offers. You may remember the USFL and the WFL. Both invested millions of dollars trying to emulate the NFL's formula. Today, each is just a distant memory.

About a year ago, I shared a river raft with Paul Tagliabue, Commissioner of the NFL, during which, unsurprisingly, the conversation turned to the world's appetite for American football. He explained it quite well, "The National Football League draws amongst the largest audiences in the world. All we do is football, so we do it very well." The individual teams (or businesses) organize themselves around the league as a central body and, together, generate revenues and earnings from a myriad of sources, including merchandise, television and licensing rights, tickets, Internet content, films, and stadium advertisements.

In late 2000, I hosted Commissioner Tagliabue, Bob Kraft, owner of the New England Patriots, and a contingent of other NFL executives who were meeting with leading Internet businesses to explore new revenue opportunities on the Web. Their agreement with Disney's ESPN for the licensing rights for NFL.com was due to expire in a few months, and they were working toward a controlled auction of the 2001/2002 Internet rights, just as they do with television rights.

Understanding that original programmed content will be available on the Web when broadband connectivity becomes more prevalent, these forward-thinking executives are one step ahead of the market's evolution. Undoubtedly, in the not-too-distant future, we will read that Internet rights are being sold at the same, if not higher, rates as television rights are today. Game day for this business runs 365 days per year.

Another business that is unwaveringly focused in its area of specialization is Staples, Inc., based in Framingham, Massachusetts. Tom Stemberg, the company's founder and chief executive officer, explained that he concentrates on offering low prices, one-stop shopping, and a broad range of products (more than 7,000). Furthermore, having a multitude of stores, including several in the same area, is crucial to his strategy. Staples now has a total of 1,100 locations, primarily in the United States, but also in Canada and Western Europe. When the chain opens a store "in Frederick, Maryland," says Stemberg, we're not just going to have one store, we're going to have two. If you want to be most convenient, you need to have the most stores." For example, in New York, Staples has 140 stores; Office Max has 40; and, Office Depot, 14. What this means, as Tom explains, is that "on average, in New York, you have to drive by seven or eight Staples stores to get to an Office Depot, or two or three to get to an Office Max. If we do a good job, nobody is going to do that, and we will win." Staples is now expanding, extending its one-stop shopping leadership onto the Internet with Staples.com, one of the market's top e-commerce destinations. When I was offered the opportunity to personally join a private financing round for Staples.com, I jumped at it. Why? Stemberg and Staples are great at what they are good at. Staples posted an amazing $8.9 billion in sales in 2000.

Achieving dominance enables a business to remain a strong leader, leaving also-rans to face prospects that are only getting tougher. Being dominant in a category has enormous benefits. For example, although eBay is down significantly from its value in early 2000—the peak of "Internet mania"—its market valuation is still over $10 billion, making it worth more than all of the world's remaining auction houses combined. Becoming synonymous with "auction," eBay has more than 10 million confirmed registered users, more people than populate the state of

Michigan. It listed 129.6 million items in 1999, compared with 33.7 million in 1998. During the fourth quarter of 1999, five people per *second* were listing items for sale on eBay, which translates into $113 of gross merchandise sales being transacted per second.

Most impressive is that its gross-merchandise sales grew an astounding 276 percent from $745 million in 1998 to $2.8 billion in 1999. With those numbers, it is not surprising to learn that users generated more economic activity on eBay than on any other consumer e-commerce site. The Web has allowed the company to create, then enhance, the category of consumer-to-consumer commerce in a way that no competitor has been able to replicate.

Several years ago, we had the opportunity to purchase eBay for less than $400 million—a bargain in today's market. Had we, I suspect the company would not now be the leader that it has become. We were not focused solely on being great at auctions. We would have been developing two emerging categories (portal and auction), simultaneously, and the likely result is that we would have done neither particularly well.

Recently, when we were in the process of launching Lycos Auctions, I met with Meg Whitman, eBay's CEO, to see if there was a way our companies could work together. I knew it would be foolhardy for Lycos to go it alone in this area because we would not be able to invest the resources that eBay, in its singular devotion to auctions, can and does. Whitman suggested that, instead, we license her technology. She was absolutely right that outsourcing the entire project was the best way to go, which is exactly what we did, although we chose an auction-infrastructure company other than eBay.

The markets don't say that only great companies will flourish in the short run. But in the long run, a great company by definition has a clearly defined core competency; and it will be able to differentiate itself, both internally and externally. Many businesses fail because they have neither. In fact, Alan Schwartz, executive vice president of the investment bank Bear Stearns, told me that "a lot of Internet companies ran their businesses based on what the market demanded for a public offering. That ruined a lot of businesses because they didn't have a vision of what it took to be a successful enterprise, they just had a goal to get financed." In other words, many Internet companies failed for good reason. They were neither great nor good at anything.

I am not referring here to what is clearly the separate issue of the stock market's valuation collapse, wherein good and bad companies lost tremendous market capitalization due to extensive panic selling. The good companies are already beginning to rebound, while the bad ones continue to fail for four basic reasons:

1. **No clear business goals:** Companies that have no plan for sustaining themselves in the long term are doomed.
2. **No customer value proposition:** It is nearly impossible to develop a revenue and earnings stream if you don't understand why your customers need your products or services.
3. **Poor execution:** Good ideas were lost as new CEOs failed to carry through the most fundamental business task—executing their plans. They were sidetracked by hype and the mad rush to liquidity.
4. **Lack of greatness anywhere:** To prosper, a business must be superb at something. It could be product design, innovation, marketing, promotion, or a combination of skills and talents. Many people thought they could slip into preexisting models and somehow imitate or recreate someone else's greatness.

Extending the concept too far, though, is also dangerous, as trying to be great at everything is a recipe for failure. As Bill

Cosby has said, "I don't know the key to success, but the key to fail-ure is trying to please everybody." Customers' diverse needs and tastes create so many niches that no one can succeed with that strategy. Far wiser is determining what you can be great at, and fo-cusing relentlessly on that. I am not suggesting that any company, especially a large one, needs to limit itself to a single area of ex-pertise. However, I do believe that it is very difficult, if not impos-sible, for a young corporation to develop multiple lines of business simultaneously and have any turn out great. Every company, re-gardless of its size, must have an in-depth expertise in at least one area in order to be viable and achieve leadership status.

This is a lesson I learned all too well. As Lycos was getting under way, I wasn't sure what the source of our long-term rev-enues would be. As a result, in an attempt to hedge our bets, we focused on two very distinct lines of business. We attempted to generate revenues as both a software-infrastructure company by licensing our search technology, and, at the same time, as a me-dia company by drawing large audiences to our Web sites and sell-ing advertising. Other companies—Infoseek, Excite, and OpenText, among them, did the same thing.

But it was problematical for us. We realized that we were not great in either area. Microsoft and AOL were becoming for-midable competitors in media, as was Inktomi in search tech-nology. Trying to be great at too many things, we failed to identify and articulate our core competencies and ended up be-ing great at nothing.

Though our revenues in each piece of the business were growing, it became clear that our business model was not going to work over time. The challenges of building a media franchise are completely different from those of creating a software com-pany. At the most basic level, the customers, products, and rele-vant employee skills are different. Fortunately, we recognized our quandary before it was too late and, after about 18 months of trial and error, we decided to build a multibrand media net-work. We learned a lesson about the importance of differentiation; we could not have achieved it without a clear and narrow focus on a single business.

Every bit as focused on performance as eBay and Staples, although very differently organized, The Limited is a company that has proven itself to be superb at building a brand. Founder and chief executive officer Leslie H. Wexner pointed out in a recent letter to shareholders that his organization is "a collection of specialty store brands. By definition, as specialists, we must be best at, must dominate, single categories that most reflect brand personalities. To do that, you have to align, and even distort, the organization to win.... That's not about averages. It's about intentionally focusing design, marketing, display, finance, stores, CEO time, everything, to win the category.... You have to be best at everything that makes the category important to the customer. How many styles? Fits? Colors? Where's the freshness?"

In marked contrast to Staples, and office-supply stores in general, The Limited is in the very "high-interest category" of women's fashions, where shoppers invest a lot of ego in their purchases. Wexner says, "Being first isn't an accident. It's deliberate. And well planned. You get focused, you make opportunities and you align the organization around them. No sideshows. We relentlessly pursue a few things, and do them very well."

Wexner's philosophy extends to all departments and every individual employee. "I expect each part of the business to focus on its expertise," he explained not long ago, on how it contributes to the brand. "I'm really not interested in what finance thinks of commercials or displays.... I want each person concentrating on what he or she can do, creatively, to add value," he continued. "Focus the resources. Relentlessly. Even maniacally. Do the things you know how to do. Do them well. And do them until they're done." If some parts of his stores are performing better than others, Wexner gets "the best store managers together" to find out how they did it.

Reflecting Wexner's ceaseless commitment to building an excellent brand, the company operates 5,000 stores throughout the U.S., which include—in addition to The Limited—Limited Too (apparel for young girls), Structure (men's clothes), The Express, Lerner New York, Lane Bryant, and Henri Bendel, among several others. In 2000, the organization posted sales of $9.7 billion.

< NEVER GET SO FOCUSED YOU LOSE FOCUS >

That General George Patton was focused on his missions is well known. Yet, he did not confuse his intense concentration with a one-dimensional view of events. The pursuit of a goal is only successful if one includes different ideas and diverse opinions. As Patton put it, "If everybody is thinking alike, then someone isn't thinking." Though Patton was speaking in a different context, he understood how essential innovation and differentiation are to success in the marketplace.

Single-mindedness that fails to anticipate changes in your business environment would be fatal. Greatness results from understanding how markets evolve. Put another way, you must define the business you are in with the utmost clarity. Consider how different the rail companies might be today had they originally defined their industry as transportation, rather than only trains. Did the early networks that defined their market as radio, rather than media, miss an opportunity?

During the early days of the personal-computer revolution, Dr. An Wang, Wang Laboratories founder and chief executive officer, told me that Wang wasn't a personal-computer company, it was a mini-computer company. But, the marketplace was changing. The computers that were about to revolutionize the industry were beginning to sit on desktops. Understandably, Wang and many other companies made the mistake of trying to protect their older and very high-gross-margin product lines at the expense of emerging technologies. Had the company considered itself great in distributed office processing, its fate may have been very different.

A company that is unswervingly focused knows what it does best, where it excels, and is not lured from its course every time a new product hits the market. Moreover, it is preoccupied with what it *is* doing, rather than what it might be doing. Yet, at the same time, that business must always be aware of what's going on outside its doors. It needs to stay abreast of emerging trends in its markets, industry, and in popular culture. In fact, the companies that can anticipate styles or behaviors before they materialize into trends are guaranteed a position at the cutting edge. In other words, the successful business sees both the forest and the trees simultaneously.

I admire Gerry Levin's (now AOL Time Warner's CEO) bold merger with America Online because it proves that companies can expand and redefine their industries. Media companies are radically transforming their models in order to accommodate the Internet. As a result, predicting the landscape of this industry just a few years from now is nearly impossible.

Though Levin and I had several discussions about the possibility of aligning our organizations, including the option of Time Warner owning a piece of Lycos, we were unable to construct a deal. Levin rightly viewed Time Warner as the dominant media company in the world, and would transact business only with an Internet company that could became the dominant online media franchise. To my disappointment, he did not feel a merger with Lycos, or any of our obvious competitors, would achieve that status. A few months later he shocked the world by selling Time Warner to AOL. The point is that his commitment to keeping his company great was so strong, he was willing to sacrifice his autonomy to participate in a merger that would ensure Time Warner's position as the leading online and offline media organization for years to come.

<CHOOSE YOUR MARKET WISELY>

If there was ever a Big Bang in the formation of the Internet, it was in April of 1994 on the day that Netscape Communications incorporated. Prior to Netscape's birth the Web remained a tool in the hands of, pretty much, the technical elite. With the advent of its browser, the Internet blossomed into something that all could master. The once-challenging concepts of bits, bytes, and a network without meaningful standards were replaced with software so simple to use that Joe Average from Main Street U.S.A. soon found himself online. Further driving the revolution was Netscape's "get big fast" strategy—it gave its browser away for free. Seemingly overnight, millions of browsers were downloaded as the company quickly established itself as the only credible interface to the online world.

If the company's launch was the Big Bang for the medium, the corollary for the feeding frenzy surrounding Internet stocks was the Netscape IPO in August 1995. Investor demand was insatiable. The stock climbed from its planned $14 to an offering price of $28 per share two days before it was set to go public and then jumped all the way to $71 with its first trade. Then, a short time later, the famed Bill Gates memo, "The Internet Tidal Wave," became public, and the rest of the world started to believe that the Internet might actually be for real. Netscape sat at the epicenter of it all.

To say the company's business model was unique might be a bit of an understatement. It gave away its product, hoping that it could capture other revenues down the road. This strategy worked quite well for a while, as Netscape became the de facto standard and watched its revenues for server and commerce software soar. What the company forgot, however, was that with revenue growth comes competition, and the sleeping Microsoft giant was soon on the prowl. With its limitless resources, Microsoft took the free model and extended it even further—beginning to give away the software that Netscape planned to charge for. It was not long before Netscape came under pressure and ultimately sold the company to AOL for an announced price of $4.2 billion in March 1999 (with the rise in AOL stock the closing price was actually closer to $9 billion).

The Netscape success is surely an amazing story by any standard. But what the story does not tell is what might have been, had the company looked at its core competencies or greatness a little differently. Netscape was a massive accumulator of "traffic," or viewers. As the Web's only viable browser, every Internet user, quite literally, traveled through the pages of Netscape. Its audience must have rivaled those of Yahoo!, AOL, Excite, and Lycos all put together. All the while, the company looked at itself as a full-services software company and continued to reject a media model as viable. This was so ingrained in the culture that even years later, Marc Andreesen, the company's cofounder told *Fast Company* magazine, ". . . if you start thinking, 'I've got lots of eyeballs and I'm going to monetize some of that traffic,' well, that's the kiss of death. . . ." In fact, Netscape even refused to build its own sales force and went so far as to subcontract its media sales efforts to a third party while it focused aggressively on software sales.

The huge opportunity that the company failed to recognize, however, is that its massive audience could have made it a massive media company with profits and margins that would rival even the best of software companies. Instead, the company chose to build its principal Web portal—Netcenter—by selling off pieces of its content pages to Lycos, Yahoo!, and others like us. With each day that this strategy remained in place, we collectively built our brands and siphoned Web users that might never visit the Netscape pages again. With their help, we were slowing and surely destroying what should have been an enduring revenue stream. Not all agreed with the Netscape approach. In particular, the Netcenter publisher at the time, Barbara Gore. I remember her continued frustrations over an inability to get the company interested in a media model. Despite soaring revenues, the company was not willing to look at itself as anything but a software provider. Barbara recognized the value of this underappreciated media asset and advocated applying the full resources of the company in building it into a market leader. Fortunately for us, her cries fell on deaf ears, and it left the portals with one less competitor to worry about. I am not quibbling with the success

Netscape enjoyed, but I suspect if it had paid a little more attention to the then uncluttered Internet media market in 1995, it
might have been the buyer of AOL or Yahoo! in 2001.

< EMBRACE RISK >

The ability to take risks is a building block of innovation and
leadership, and those who shy away from them are rarely successful. With risks come mistakes, which every great company
has experienced; they are part of the process of building a business. With plenty of experience building and reinvigorating
businesses, Disney's chairman and chief executive officer
Michael Eisner believes that "when you're trying to create
things that are new, you have to be prepared to be on the edge
of risk." The truth is, "We're all paid to take risks."

There is a story of a wise old businessman who is address-
ing his employees when a new hire raises his hand and asks,
"How did you become such a great business leader?" The old man
answers, "with great business decisions." The employee asks him
how he learned to make great decisions, to which the older man
answers "experience." When the persistent employee asks, "How
did you gain experience?" The old man replies, "bad decisions."

Risk is ingrained in the fabric of any successful culture.
Explorers from Lewis and Clark to Neil Armstrong, physicists
from Galileo to Einstein, scientists such as Curie and Salk all
contributed to the continuation of humanity. Risk takers extra-
ordinaire, they are part of our legacy.

Similarly, the entrepreneurs of the last 150 years have
taken substantial risks to create technologies and systems that
have influenced, perhaps determined, aspects of contemporary
life. Think of a world without the work of Bell, Edison, and Andy
Grove. If achieving greatness was not each man's original goal,
it was certainly his result. Innovation rarely occurs without risk,
which means accepting setbacks. Expressing the perseverance
inherent in accomplishment, Thomas Edison wrote: "I speak

without exaggeration when I say I have constructed 3,000 different theories in connection with the electric light, yet in only two cases did my experiments prove the truth of my theory." Like the fabled old businessman, Edison is telling us that learning from our past mistakes will help us succeed.

When aspiring managers ask successful executives for a single piece of advice, frequently, they answer with a variation on this: Never say you don't know how to do something. Accept the responsibility, then learn whatever it is.

Risk should not be confused with recklessness. Time Warner's Gerald Levin, for example, has long discerned the difference. Before the AOL merger, no combination of old and new media had been successful. Though he was an outspoken proponent of new media, his challenge to his company has been to pursue creative risk-taking and is directed consistently throughout his organization. In a recent speech, he pointed out that not everyone is comfortable with this, and added, "From the culturally correct on the right to the politically correct on the left, there are any number of groups pressuring the media to stick to a preapproved script." But, Levin said, a free world depends on media that "refuse to be intimidated into blind conformity, steering clear of creative risk in the hope of avoiding controversy."

Charles Schwab, another smart risk taker, is once again on *Fortune*'s list of most admired companies. A consistent innovator in the conservative financial-services industry, Schwab was the first company, in 1982, to offer free IRA accounts, in 1985 the first to offer a software trading product; and the first to go online in 1996. Schwab's founder, the company's namesake, is proud of his willingness to overlook what are referred to in the company as "noble failures" in order to deliver the robust innovations that have propelled his company into its leadership role in the brokerage business. Schwab knows that people who "introduce new ideas ... have to be able to take a lot of ridicule. If ... you undermine the bad ideas, no one will ever want to come up with a good one. And if 50 percent of them work, that's pretty damn good."

CMGI is another risk taker that has over a period of time delivered solid results to its shareholders. Notwithstanding the conflicts between Lycos and CMGI that I discussed in chapter 3, Dave Wetherell, the company's founder, should be credited for his courage to fund Web-related ideas and businesses, when, in the early 1990s, the Internet was a very new frontier. In 1994 when Wetherell was CEO of his direct-marketing organization, he had the foresight to envision the Web's potential. He put together a team to develop a Web browser that would help publishers get their content online. The result was Booklink, a company which Wetherell later sold to America Online for 710,000 shares of AOL stock, valued, at that time, at $70 million—a substantial windfall in 1994.

Though many people would have laid back with such a gain, Wetherell used virtually all of the proceeds to fund the first Internet-only venture-capital fund. He hired Dan Nova from Summit Partners; Jerry Colonna, editor-in-chief of *Information Week*, now a partner at Flatiron Ventures; and a team of other professionals to find and place long-term strategic bets on startups in their initial stage. It was a bold, high-risk bet. In addition to Lycos, the group invested in companies with no history, names like Vicinity, Freemail, Black Sun, ThingWorld, and dozens of others. When, shortly thereafter, Internet growth skyrocketed, CMGI's gamble began to pay its shareholders huge dividends. From an IPO market capitalization of $23 million in 1994, the company soared in value, and, in early 2001, despite a frightening free fall from its levels a few months before, was worth more than 65 times that. In this case, taking a risk to realize a bold vision produced one of the most rapid ascents in the history of public venture capital.

< LEARN FROM THE LEADER >

Looking for greatness wherever we go is a helpful habit. Leaders are often models for greatness, and an examination of their practices provides valuable insights. For instance, no discussion of companies that are great at what they're good at would be complete without Dell Computer. Dell's innovative way of transacting business has become its hallmark, and deservedly so. The people at Dell call it the *direct business model*, and following it to greatness is what the company credits for its extraordinary growth. When, in the early 1990s, Dell placed all of its internal technical materials online, the customer response was overwhelmingly positive. Online service opened new avenues for support and sales and resulted in huge savings for Dell, compared to the costs of providing the same services over the telephone. Online support saved about $5 per customer interaction, bringing the cumulative savings into the millions.

Today, Dell generates over $40 million in sales every day of the year through its online sites, and has became a *Fortune* 100 company. Michael Dell, the company's founder, chairman, and chief executive officer, was among the first to understand and capture the potential opportunities of e-commerce. He focused his business around those openings while most people were ignoring them. Virtually all of my conversations with him have centered on his plans to expand his customer relationships by entering new and emerging areas. To this day, Dell remains great at what it is good at.

< NEVER LET UP ON QUALITY >

Maintaining your passion for greatness is a commandment held sacred by any successful business. But as Jack Welch says, "Managing success is a tough job. There's a very fine line between self-confidence and arrogance. Success often breeds both, along with reluctance to change. The bureaucracy builds up. The people start to believe they're invulnerable. Before they know it, the world changes, and they've got to react."

Intel's chairman Andy Grove is another believer in the stay-great ethos. Founded over 30 years ago, Intel's initial goal was to build an alternative to what was then the dominant computer memory technology and make it cheaper and better. Since Andy Grove, Robert Noyce, and Gordon Moore started the company, it has grown into the world's largest chip maker, and currently powers approximately 80 percent of the world's desktop computers, generating over $30 billion a year in revenues.

Intel's record is the best expression of its commitment to remaining a leader in innovative technology. It delivered the 8080 processor in 1974; the 286, 386, and 486 processors in 1982, 1985, and 1989, respectively; the Pentium in 1983; and the Pentium Xeon in 1998.

Millions of people in every part of the world use Intel chips in networks to form our global information systems. Moreover, microprocessors are now a part of every imaginable device—automobiles, toys, cellular phones, refrigerators, and coffeemakers. They change the way we live, work, and entertain.

< PUSH HARDER >

Being great at what you're good at isn't simple. First and foremost, you have to decide exactly what it is you're good at. Then you must relinquish everything that isn't directly related to promoting your success. You need to push relentlessly for excellence, which includes staying on top of, and in touch with, your markets, changes in technologies, and your customers. You have to inspire your employees; master the art of negotiating the deal; and learn from stellar performers in other fields. Then, just when you think you have finally made it, take a deep breath, find your second wind, and push a little harder.

8

Every moment with a customer
is a moment of

truth

Every moment with a customer is a moment of truth

MY FIRST EXPERIENCE with the power of quality customer service dates back more than 25 years. I was working in a supermarket and one day an irate customer berated me about the length of the checkout line. The supermarket manager overheard her, but didn't get involved in the argument—he simply took a ten-cent candy bar and dropped it into the woman's bag.

"I know the line was long today," he said. "We apologize, and we hope you'll come back."

The woman's attitude instantly changed from hostility to surprised gratitude. With a very small gesture, the supermarket manager turned a negative experience into a pleasant memory and won a loyal customer. For just ten cents, he bought a lifetime of goodwill.

That was a moment of truth—and a good employee seized it to create a positive experience for a customer. In any business, moments of truth occur dozens, hundreds, or even thousands of times a day. Our attitudes and behavior at these moments determine the customer's experience. Happy customers will champion your company's virtues, while angry ones will tell one and all that you betrayed their trust. Doing the right thing is a cardinal rule.

Almost every company is quick to declare its commitment to customer satisfaction. But do they behave that way? Many don't. They simply don't invest the resources and undertake the training that is needed to turn a motto into a mission. If you tell a new hire, "Customers come first at this company," and then during his first week on the job that employee sees an action that contradicts what you've told him—well, you've got two problems: A disillusioned employee and an unhappy customer.

A good example of responding to the customer opportunity comes from the insurance company USAA. A few years ago, customer service representative Stephanie Valadez answered a call from a distraught elderly woman. The widow of a military officer, she was calling USAA in the midst of an ice storm in upstate New York that had knocked out her power. She told Valadez that she was ill, had run out of her medicine, and was freezing in her unheated house. Her husband, who had trusted the insurance company implicitly, advised her to call USAA if she was ever in a desperate situation. "He said you would take care of me." With the woman on hold, Valadez called the Red Cross, relayed all the relevant information, and arranged for them to visit her the same day.

But the story doesn't end there. As soon as the caller identified herself, Valadez accessed her file and discovered that she had let the policy lapse following her husband's death. Valadez knew all along that the person she was helping was no longer a customer. As a company executive points out, "I suspect that most other companies would have hung up on her, but hanging up isn't part of our mind-set. That's what we mean when we say that customer service is a relationship, not a transaction."

Our days teem with opportunities to win customers. Too often they're just ignored. Do any of the following sound familiar?
- You're sitting in a meeting with a delegation from one of your suppliers. You ask a question and the response is, "We'll get back to you." But no one jots anything down. In

reality, you know, "get back to you" means: "Why bother to ask such an unimportant question; I don't know the answer, let's forget about it." That all-too-frequent exchange always amazed me, because if there's ever an opportunity to create a moment of truth, that is it.

It's called follow-through. An employee who ignores directives from his or her superior isn't likely to remain employed very long. Why should that behavior be acceptable when dealing with the most important boss of all—customers? *Every* customer question demands a timely, professional, and helpful response.

- How many times have you called a company, left message after message, and not had your call returned? There's no excuse. Developing a system that ensures 100-percent responsiveness is just good business.
- Corporate buck-passing, or the ability to transfer responsibility for a problem, is one of the more common atrocities. A customer calls with a concern, question, complaint, even a compliment. The employee on the phone says that handling it isn't his job and tells the customer to call someone else. It's amazing how often this occurs, especially when you think about how easy it is to do the right thing. Whoever answers the phone should simply say, "Thank you for calling. I understand your issue, and I'll arrange for someone to get back to you promptly." Then follow through: Take responsibility, find the right department and person, relay the call, and make sure it's returned. It's a lot easier for an employee to wind his or her way through an organization's bureaucracy than it is for a customer, and it should be expected behavior. When you ask someone to call back, you risk losing that person in the frustrating netherworld of voice mail. So much of customer service is basic human courtesy and kindness, as that supermarket manager taught me 25 years ago. Keep it simple.

If you regularly commit the three *very* avoidable blunders described above, you may well be committing slow business suicide. When it's time to renew a contract, buy a product, or offer a recommendation, that customer won't be there. Blowing that moment of truth may be just enough to blow away that order.

For an Internet media company like Lycos, there are three core customers. Each is important, but the most prized is the one who pays nothing and remains faceless—the users. Without them, you have nothing—no ads to sell, no commerce to promote, and no employees to pay. Without their loyalty you can't survive.

Lycos had 91 million users a month, nearly all of whom remained loyal without ever speaking to us. Our lifeblood was this anonymous constituency that we served each and every day. Our moments of truth often came without immediate or visible feedback. They resulted from the quality of the products, the professionalism of our teams, and the ability of our employees to convey to these unseen masses just how highly regarded they were.

The second core customer group was our paying partners. These are the easiest for most of us to understand and appreciate. The client that buys the audience we painstakingly built. Suffice to say that if someone is paying you they better like the way they're being treated.

Finally, our employees were our customers. Every employee was the client of every other employee. We all worked for and relied upon each other to make the business a success. Individuals want to feel valued, so it's essential that the concept of the employee-as-customer be built into corporate values and culture.

Not long ago, I served with the legendary Herb Kelleher, chairman and CEO of Southwest Airlines, on a committee to select *Chief Executive* magazine's CEO of the year. His focus on the customer was clear and passionate. This is probably why his company is as well known for its employees' humor and light touch, as it is for its low fare "no frills" flights. Southwest Airlines recognizes its employees, according to Herb, "as human beings—not just people who work for our company.... We have not been prescriptive as to how people can or should behave when they're on the job. Fundamentally, they can behave the way that their basic natures influence them to behave." As a leader, Kelleher, who has "fun" spending time with the mechanics and baggage handlers, wants people to "feel valued for who they are, to feel good about themselves and good about what they do, [which] . . . also gives vent to their creative energies, their imaginations." The result is relaxed and happy employees who treat customers like friends.

Lycos' approach to satisfying the end-user embodied a paradox. People came to us for help navigating the Web, but measured their success by how quickly they could leave: They arrived, searched, found the sought-for site, then left. Obviously, the quick departure undermined our goal of selling a large audience to advertisers, and we weren't alone in this hold-the-customer challenge.

A customer comes into Macy's, for instance, for many reasons—a sale, to browse, or for a specific purchase. The store spends untold hours strategizing and planning its layout, with the goal of keeping customers in the store for as long as possible, so that they spend as much money as possible. However, smart retailers know that customers can't be locked in a maze with no escape until their wallets are empty. Even if this works once, that customer won't return. The shopping experience should be fun, entertaining, and designed so that the customer *wants* to stay. Macy's layout, while intended to keep you a little bit longer, pays scrupulous attention to ensuring that you enjoy being there. We did the same online.

This pleasure principle applies to all businesses. You may score a sale using pressure, trickery, or "act-before-midnight-tonight" tactics—but the only way to build genuine loyalty is to reward the customer with an experience that is second-to-none.

To serve your customers you have to understand them. At Lycos we continually used new tools to help us do so. We conducted online surveys and held focus groups, sometimes lasting for weeks, that helped us construct a product to customer specifications. When we put together a new service, we sought feedback. We asked users detailed questions on color, format, speed, ease—what they liked and didn't like—and we changed the product accordingly.

Each week, we invited groups of consumers to a usability laboratory, where we had sophisticated devices that measured their interactions with our products. We used computer technology to track eyeball movement. This equipment measures precisely how someone reads a computer screen so that editors and designers can compose pages more effectively.

There's no single formula that will produce high-quality customer experiences; dozens of variables enter the equation. About three years ago, we realized that our Web pages were slow to respond. We measured precisely how long it took users to log onto our site: We clicked onto Lycos.com from hundreds of points around the country, timed how long it took for the page to appear, and then compared our average with our competitors. Though this wasn't the only measurement of customer satisfaction, it was an important one. We had a rich, interesting site, but it took several seconds longer to download than our competitors' sites. I had no doubt that this was costing us customers. Others, by contrast, were simple, graphically pleasing, and lightning fast.

The issue triggered heated debate at Lycos. Our engineers said the page had too many graphics to download quickly. The designers said we didn't have the right network architecture. The network architects said the engineers hadn't designed strong enough software. And the people in marketing were blaming all of the above.

But everyone put their differences aside, focused on the customer, and worked together to solve the problem. We limited the graphics, condensed the page, and delivered a faster experience. Today, Lycos consistently remains among the top companies in this critical category.

Offering an immediate response to customer criticism is a given. But anticipating a need before it becomes a complaint, as we did when we sped up access to our Web pages, is even better.

Lycos customers viewed us as their personal Internet guide or even as their own research assistant. This is an image we worked hard to establish. As a result, we received all kinds of queries. One woman wanted to know where she could see a specific species of endangered monkeys; someone else wanted to find a brand of peanut butter that his local stores no longer stocked; and one person needed help getting rid of an army of ants that was marching across her kitchen floor.

We were happy to answer all and any requests to the best of our ability. But with the overwhelming volume it was important to develop solutions that put technology to good use.

There's a classic story from the early twentieth century about a man who was bitten by bedbugs in a Pullman car, and complained in a letter to the president of the Pullman Company. The president wrote back that he was shocked to hear of this problem, which was unprecedented and intolerable; he had fired all those who were responsible, and the condition would never again occur. Sounds great, except that the customer's original letter of complaint was inadvertently included with the reply. Scrawled across the top was: "Mildred, send him the bedbug letter."

The sheer volume of correspondence today makes the "bedbug" or form letter necessary. But, with technology and smart software, we can send form letters that are nearly as personalized as a handwritten note.

There are dozens of customer-relationship management systems available in the market, which not only provide automatic e-mail systems, but are capable of extensive customization. Employees at Lycos can screen each message and cue the customized reply with a few keystrokes. The messages are direct and informal, yet each looks very personal.

< P R A C T I C E W H A T Y O U P R E A C H >

Total and genuine commitment to the customer should permeate every level of an organization. The chief executive of Ritz-Carlton personally conducts employee orientation at each new property. The owners of Nordstrom continue to walk the floors, speak with customers, and help at check-out counters. At many Veterans Administration Medical Centers, patients being admitted are welcomed personally by the local director. This kind of top-down commitment has a ripple effect throughout an organization.

My obsession with the customer experience was a good-natured joke at Lycos. At least once a week, usually on a Friday or Saturday night, I logged on to the network for a few hours. I clicked through the pages and looked to see if anything was malfunctioning, awkward, or out of context. In the course of being logged on, I typically sent out two dozen or so e-mails to employees reporting problems. Micro-management? Maybe, but if the CEO isn't fully engaged, how can he or she expect the company to be?

Our mission statement at Lycos was: "To become the most visited online destination in the world by winning people's time with the best interactive products and a customer focus that is second-to-none." The operative word—"winning"—conveyed our dual essence: first, the intensity that we had become so proud of, and second, the concept that customers have a choice.

In my orientation briefing to new employees, I laid out our challenge. To start, out of all the options in a person's busy life, a consumer must decide to log on. Once online, there are some one billion Web sites to choose from. Rather daunting odds. We won because we were able to differentiate ourselves—we were faster, our graphics were more attractive, our information was better, our communities were stronger. The bottom line was that we had to win hearts and minds. Once viewed in this context, organizations can motivate their employees in remarkable ways.

Ours is a society that loves a good fight, and instilling that concept of competition into your company's culture will always serve you well. And there's no better place to demonstrate that ethos in action than at the top.

<SERVE THE CUSTOMER>

I've learned a lot about customers from my own experiences as one. Dealing with Netscape was particularly instructive on how not to treat a client. In my view, Netscape had grown big, bold, and arrogant. Though I was paying them $5 million a year, I always left meetings feeling that they expected me to be grateful that they'd accepted my money.

Netscape should have been a big winner on the Internet. At one point, it owned 90 percent of the browser market; you couldn't pick up *Forbes, Fortune*, or *Business Week* without reading how it was conquering the Web. But its corporate attitude slowly but surely turned many in the industry against it. That this was happening at a time when Microsoft was the company many loved to hate spoke even more to the problem. It was Microsoft that many in the industry rooted for to win the browser competition.

No one will deny that Netscape was a pioneer and achieved great success, but it forgot about the customer, which marked the beginning of its end. Ultimately, AOL acquired Netscape for about $4 billion, obviously not a small sum, but probably a fraction of what its value could have been.

The lesson is that it's not only the amount of attention you pay a customer, but the quality. Nancy Kramer, president and CEO of Resource Marketing, Inc., recently remarked that "every client I talk to says the same thing: 'We want to own the customer.' But when it comes to the Web, you can't own customers unless you earn them."

So learn humility. Do what you say you'll do, and, if you can't do it, don't promise you will. Kramer found some egregious offenders on the Web. For example, sites that invite you to ask about their product, but include a disclaimer that they can't answer every question they receive.

On the other hand, Kramer has found sites—a bookseller is one—that she loves. The mother of three, she asked for information on children's books. The e-mail response "was written in a way that felt personal, as if they were paying special attention just to me." Furthermore, they notified her that a particular author, whose books she has ordered in the past, had a new one coming out. There are many ways to convey the same information, but the bookseller did it in a way that Kramer, a sophisticated consumer, found "friendly" and, perhaps, most important, "nonintrusive."

The root of the word "service" is "servant." Anyone creating a site today should think of himself or herself in just that way. You have to be humble, considerate, and able to anticipate needs. It has been said a million times before, but it is one of those business basics that can never be said too often: You have to earn customers' trust and confidence. Until you do, you will never own them.

<BUILD A CULTURE COMMITTED TO THE CUSTOMER>

Making customers feel valued requires a company-wide commitment. Some businesses, investment banking among them, are based almost entirely on the quality of the relationship between the banker and the customer. Since an investment bank can perform many functions, the scope of its responsibilities is often determined by the extent to which the client trusts the judgment and character of the banker.

I've worked with many over the last few years, and all have served me well, yet none better than Allen & Company. The firm's obvious high regard for its employees was a revelation and an inspiration. In an industry where tenure rarely extends beyond a few years, Allen has developed a team that has stayed together for decades. It has a collegial atmosphere that clearly recognizes its employees as its customers, which works to the benefit of its clients.

My first encounter with the company occurred in 1999 during the Lycos and USA chaos. Jack Schneider, head of institutional sales at Allen arranged for me to make a series of presentations to institutional investors. As a result, despite the fact that the USA deal was aborted, I met many people who remain shareholders today. Jack wasn't a banker on the deal. He helped because it was a moment of truth, and he seized it. I have come to be friends with Jack, and his ability to make his clients feel respected and important is unmatched.

Another company that has woven a culture of service deep into its fabric is L. L. Bean. The billion-dollar Maine retailer has been in business for nearly a hundred years. Its founder, Leon Leonwood Bean created an environment where "do unto others" wasn't just a phrase, but a way of life. When he launched his first Maine Hunting shoe store in 1912, he set out his mission.

> *The Golden Rule*
> Sell good merchandise at a reasonable
> profit, treat your customers like human
> beings, and they will always
> come back for more.

Now, almost a century later, the company continues to measure success by the satisfaction of its customers. It proudly proclaims a 100 percent guarantee in its catalogs and on its Web sites: "If unsatisfied, return anything purchased from us at any time. We will replace it, refund your purchase price, or credit your credit card. We do not want you to have anything from L. L. Bean that is not completely satisfactory."

The very notion of a customer returning a product at any time, potentially years after it was purchased, would strike terror in the hearts of many retailers. At L. L. Bean, it's a proud differentiation.

John Chambers, CEO of Cisco Systems, describes the customer-retailer relationship as "partners for life." In the summer of 2000, I was in Madrid having dinner with Juan Villalonga, chairman of the Spanish phone giant Telefónica. Over dessert, Villalonga explained the value he places on partnerships. The example he used was Cisco. He said that on closing their first deal together, Chambers shook his hand and pronounced them "partners for life." The effect of this gesture on Villalonga was so profound that, years later and half a world away, he continued to repeat the story.

‹MAKE YOUR EMPLOYEES EVANGELISTS›

At Lycos, I urged employees to arrive each morning vowing to make something better for a customer or colleague. By recognizing that every interaction was a moment of truth, our employees became a powerful grassroots force.

Perhaps no company reflects this attitude more than the Walt Disney Company. They have done a superlative job turning its work force into an army of goodwill agents. Anyone who has visited its theme parks is familiar with the employees' graciousness. Their smiles don't seem forced, they make every visitor feel welcome, and the service is superb. This positive, can-do approach is ingrained in the company's culture. But it didn't get there by accident.

Vice president and general manager in Disney's vacation development office George Aguel credits founder Walt Disney for setting a core set of values based on service, quality, creativity, and leadership. As relevant in the twenty-first century as it was 50 years ago, this code of ethics remains the axis around which the entire organization revolves. And turning employees into passionate evangelists of the company's mission is one of its key elements.

< CAPITALIZE ON MOMENTS OF TRUTH >

At the end of the day, treating customers well requires more art than science—and more common sense than either. Nevertheless, I have found a few rules to be particularly helpful:

When your customer tells you something, listen

Since the days of Socrates, dialogue has been the most effective vehicle for understanding our fellow humans, a.k.a. customers. Dick Egan, chairman of EMC, told me that it's impossible to overstate the importance of dialogue. "You have to engage the customers so that they feel comfortable telling you what problems they have and what they're trying to accomplish, so that you can try to turn those problems into solutions."

Gateway 2000 is another company that understands the value of listening. Ted Waite, the company's founder, kept me enthralled one night as he passionately expounded on his belief that the customer *is* the company and that *nothing* is more important than an ongoing dialogue. His senior vice president of global marketing, Jim Taylor, makes a fine distinction between "relating" to a product and simply "using" it. Taylor urges companies to appreciate "that the aesthetic experience people have with products and services are just as important as conventional measures of quality and performance."

How can an Internet company, a clothing store, or any business, on- or offline, understand how customers *really* relate to a product? How can they measure the subtle, emotional connection, if in fact one exists? Through dialogue. Taylor believes that customers view companies as "corrupt, unresponsive, unavailable," and that they feel this way even if, at the same time, they're using and liking the company's products.

This is provocative thinking, and a reality that few executives are willing to acknowledge to themselves, much less discuss with others. It is incumbent that companies build a "communications pipeline" that will facilitate honest dialogue among managers, other employees, and customers.

Taylor has ensured that communications pipelines flow freely in his company: "When we launch a new product, we identify . . . 'early adopters' . . . and christen them 'pioneers.' We talk to them . . . find out what's working and not working."

Whenever the engineers find and fix bugs, they upgrade the pioneers' machines for free. The result is "a sustained dialogue that benefits both sides." Pioneers have fun and earn free upgrades and the company's engineers can track how people use the machines they have made.

Perhaps most significantly, the relationships create "positive energy from the sheer pleasure" of sharing exciting discoveries with interesting people.

In business, nothing is more important than the customer. It may sound like the ultimate no-brainer, but you would be shocked how often it's forgotten. After all, running a business sometimes feels like juggling six balls while racing on a treadmill. That *everyone* loses sight of the customer now and then might not be forgivable but it is certainly understandable. That's why constant reminders are in order, because the day that we stop talking to our customers is the day it all comes tumbling down. An honest dialogue is what keeps us one step ahead.

Use the Web to your advantage

A quality Web site has become a necessity for nearly every business, whether you run a hardware store or manufacture jet engines. As a customer, I take it for granted that I can click on a site and learn about products, prices, delivery times, even warehouse locations and shipping procedures. Sites also communicate point of view, culture, tone.

Many companies use their Web sites to provide information to their supply chain; they post specifications for bids, and make their own order books available so that suppliers can arrange their production schedules accordingly.

But having a Web site is a two-edged sword. If you have a site only because you think you have to, you've made a big mistake. A site that fails to fulfill expectations is tantamount to advertising your incompetence. Many savvy businesspeople underestimate the complexity of designing a Web site and setting up the infrastructure. The Christmas 1999 Toys 'R' Us site exemplifies the risks of a poorly designed site. The company promoted and then launched its site before it was equipped to handle shoppers. As a result, customers either couldn't connect, or, if they did, couldn't navigate. They found products out of stock and couldn't find items that they knew were in the stores. That season the company could rightly be called Toys 'R'nt Us.

The lesson: In many ways, your Web site *is* your company. Make sure it lives up to that challenge.

Customers remember failures—don't disappoint them

It's almost impossible to undo an unfavorable impression; it lingers long after you've cured the problem that triggered it.

Among the challenges I faced during my years at Wang was the company's deserved reputation for poor customer service. Though the company had grown dramatically, customer service hadn't kept pace. Management belatedly addressed the problem by hiring new executives, overhauling logistics systems, and focusing employees on service. Still, years later, when Wang had one of the best programs in the industry, its poor reputation endured, and revenue growth was stymied by the market's perception that it remained unreliable.

Stanley Marcus, chairman emeritus of the Neiman Marcus Company, inherited the business from his father—and never forgot the lessons he learned from him. As he wrote in a recent issue of *Fast Company*: "My father wanted people to be happy. He knew that a customer wouldn't be happy if she bought the wrong item. For that reason, he would always take things back—even if they had been worn or abused. In the long run, this approach helped us build a clientele that is second to none in customer loyalty." Put another way, no matter what you sell, you've got to sell satisfaction.

Early in Marcus's career, when he was working in the fur department, his father pointed to a black broadtail coat that cost $6,000 and told him "to find a customer for it," which he did. The son was beaming when his father happened to stop by the fur department the following week as the woman was having her new coat fitted. But his father quickly pulled him aside and told him he had made a big mistake.

The senior Marcus, who often saw the woman in the store, knew that she sold life insurance and carried a large leather shoulder bag filled with heavy policies. The tug of the bag would quickly wear out the fur on the shoulder of the coat. Marcus assured his father that he had warned her that it was a fragile fur. Senior Marcus patiently explained to his son that while she might understand that now, she wouldn't be so accepting on the day the coat started coming apart.

"That little black broadtail coat was the most difficult fur I've ever had to sell, and certainly the only one that I've ever had to un-sell," Marcus remembered. "But I realized that you can't sell satisfaction if you give people the wrong advice. Give people the wrong advice, and they'll never forgive you."

At Disney, customer delight is a way of life. What I call moments of truth the people at Disney call magic moments. I experienced one firsthand. When my oldest son was two years old, my wife and I took him for a vacation to Disney World in Orlando, Florida. Our first day at the park was fabulous. My son met a bevy of Disney characters and had a wonderful adventure. Day two was a different story. We returned to our hotel around noon to find his favorite stuffed animal and "lifelong companion," Puffy, missing. Every parent understands that this is a serious trauma. He sobbed himself to sleep as I frantically phoned housekeeping for help with our "crisis." Within minutes they had delivered a replacement—a stuffed Disney character—and assured me that the search would continue. It seemed as though Disney mobilized the entire company to find our missing friend. Guest services, housekeeping, and the front desk were all in on the operation. It turned out that Puffy had been loaded up with linens and made his way to the company's laundry facility several miles away. An observant employee spotted the little guy and personally drove back to our hotel. Disney truly turned a moment of truth into a magical moment.

When it comes to service, one size does not fit all

Customer service must stay flexible, fluid, adaptive. Rigid customer service is an oxymoron, yet many companies continue to codify it, unwilling to put a little power in the hands of those on the front line—or just plain unwilling to spend the time and money customized solutions demand. Our culture and economy influence customer expectations as well. Today, customers expect to have many more choices than they did 20 years ago.

Service is important in every industry, but perhaps nowhere is it as crucial as in the restaurant business. Restaurateur Danny Meyer, president of Union Square Hospitality Group, made an interesting distinction between "customer service" and "hospitality, in an article he wrote for *Fast Company*. Meyer considers customer service a "technical skill"—the food arrives on time, the wine is presented properly, plates are cleared gracefully and promptly.

Hospitality, on the other hand, transcends mere customer service and offers an emotional benefit. When you leave a restaurant you feel "that the staff is on your side." For example, a server overhears you saying that you can't decide between two dishes—and so he or she brings you a small sampling of each.

Or say you accidentally leave your sunglasses on the table. When you call, you're told to come pick them up anytime. Meyer's group responds differently. They immediately ask where you would like the sunglasses sent and then a messenger—or even FedEx—is dispatched. Obviously this costs money, but

Meyer considers it a sound investment. He feels that when a customer has to go back to a restaurant to retrieve a forgotten item, it subtly sullies the whole dining experience. What's remembered may not be the terrific meal, but the hassle of going back. That's a strong example of being on the customer's side.

Meyer and his people understand that every diner is different, and they understand the emotional component of their product. And so they tailor their agenda to the customer, not the other way around.

"People don't want to feel that they're at your mercy, especially on board an airplane," Yap Kim Wah, senior vice president of marketing services at Singapore Airlines, Ltd., explained in a recent article, "so we give them a wide selection of choices—from what and when they eat to how and when they are entertained."

Like many of the executives and employees I've cited in this chapter, Yap Kim Wah emphasizes the need to treat each person as an individual. It "means doing the little things, looking for opportunities to provide extra . . . care. It means making passengers feel as if everything you do were especially for them."

On a recent Singapore Airlines flight, a wailing baby was making everyone miserable. The infant kept dropping his pacifier. Flight attendants, his parents, and even passengers would join in the search for the rolling object—anything to stop that screaming. Finally, an inspired attendant attached the pacifier to a ribbon, and sewed it onto the child's shirt. The surrounding passengers gave the attendant a standing ovation.

That's the kind of adaptive customer service that all companies should strive for. Remember that everyone is different and every circumstance is different, remember the emotional component—and then deliver customized satisfaction.

Adopt a zero-tolerance policy

It's *never* acceptable to disappoint a customer. Corporations that set standards of, say, 98-percent customer satisfaction are shameful. How do they explain to the 2 percent that their dissatisfaction is acceptable? Seek less than perfection and that's what you'll get. In Lycos' early days, computer and network failures weren't unusual in the industry, but that didn't change the fact that they made our services unavailable to users. When an operations executive presented a plan to guarantee 95-percent availability, I fired him. And, to this day, I don't understand his reasoning.

Since then, the Lycos Network achieved 100-percent availability, for which I credit a passionate team that refused to accept anything short of excellence. If your standards accept mediocrity, you will rarely achieve anything better. Although there are always variables beyond our control, and we humans are, by definition, imperfect, if your standards demand the best, you might not reach it every time—but then again, you might. And the striving will make your organization strong and a sure leader in its marketplace.

My emphasis, at the heart of each of these rules, is your need to capitalize on customer moments of truth. A moment of truth can be as complex as an order-processing infrastructure or as simple as a ten-cent candy bar. Either way, if you seize that moment and do the right thing, you will win new customers and keep old ones loyal for a lifetime.

People are your

foundation

9

IN THE SUMMER OF 1999, I met with John McMahon in an attempt to convince him to leave his position with a large multi-national and join Lycos as senior vice president of human resources. Up until then, I had only known him from afar as a man of impeccable credentials. He quickly took control of our interview and laid down McMahon's Law of Human Resources: "Neither I nor my team plan picnics and outings; we build careers and top notch organizations." With those 16 words I knew he was our man. Why? Because he understood—as the title of this chapter suggests—that the employees are the foundation on which a successful business is built. People, not products, build companies.

It's that simple. Arm the right people with a hard challenge, a flexible culture, peers they admire, and fair compensation and they can take on the world. Inspire people to believe in their own worth. Teach them to expect victory. Free them to excel. Then stand back and watch the bonanza of winning products, loyal customers, happy directors, and delighted investors.

Carly Fiorina, CEO of Hewlett-Packard, knows that "the greatest strategy . . . the greatest financial plan . . . the greatest turnaround in the world" are only temporary if they aren't "grounded in people." Albert Einstein had to remind himself "a hundred times every day" that his accomplishments were "based on the labors of others." Every businessperson should do the same.

Good people attract other good people, and before long you have a unique group of dedicated, passionate employees—the human spark that ignites the corporate spirit.

In this chapter, I detail eight concepts—"people principles"—that I find indispensable. Vignettes from a wide variety of companies demonstrate the principles' relevance to any business.

< HIRING WELL IS JOB ONE >

No managerial task is more important to do well than hiring—and none is more harmful when done badly. Haste is often enemy number one. It's one of the biggest, and most avoidable, mistakes you can make. I remember an executive at Wang instructing new managers to get "warm bodies" into the company at any cost. "Hire people now!" he told them. "Fix the problems later!" Employees aren't "wam bodies." They are the soul of an organization. You succeed or fail based on the collective abilities and talents of your team. Hiring well is a discipline that requires diligence, patience, and passion.

In order to enrich the organization, you have to have a *comprehensive* understanding of who you need and why and where. You're not just filling a slot; you're bringing in a unique new individual who will have a ripple effect on all those around her. So don't rush to judgment. Study the cultural and personal qualities that unify or divide a group or team. Consider chemistry. Excluding the social consequences and business disruption of a poor hiring decision, one need look only at the economic ramifications. The fully loaded cost of a typical employee in a professional environment is about $125,000 per year. Most well-run businesses have an extensive system of checks and balances in place to ensure that any $125,000 decision is made properly. Yet, far too many of these same businesses allow

$125,000 hiring decisions to be made recklessly. It is also staggering how quickly the financial impact accumulates. Envision a company hiring perhaps 150 employees in a given year; surely a modest number to many corporations. If just 10 percent of these hires are poorly executed, the cost to the company is $1,875,000 in the first year alone. Of course, it is very short-sighted to look at this solely in regards to the economic impact. The real "costs" to the business relate to the success of the company itself.

Herb Kelleher, CEO of Southwest Airlines, believes that rushing through the hiring process never fails to provoke messy, complex, and time-consuming problems that outweigh the inconvenience of a prolonged search. Kelleher was delighted when a slightly embarrassed vice president of his "People Department" admitted that her office had interviewed 34 people for a ramp agent position in Amarillo, Texas, without finding the right fit. His response: "If you have to interview 134 people to get the right attitude on the ramp in Amarillo, Texas, do it."

Bad hiring patterns are like a blaring smoke alarm—they indicate fire ahead. And while you never want to hire in haste, it is equally important that a proper balance be struck. Hiring can never be put on a back burner. How often have you encountered a manager who exclaims, "I am too busy to source candidates, sort resumes, interview candidates..." Not keeping up with the staffing needs of the company is a certain path to difficulties. Managers whose work load is far outstripping their ability to fill open job requisitions need help. Sooner or later, this imbalance will cause a key process, or even a whole company, to break down. When you don't have enough good people to get the job done, it's inevitable that those carrying the load will become angry, frustrated, and dissatisfied. Eventually, you lose them, leaving lazy managers and a sloppy company in the lurch.

Jeff Bezos, Amazon.com's founder and CEO, says it well. "Setting the bar high...has been, and will continue to be, the single most important element of Amazon.com's success. During hiring meetings, we ask people to consider three questions before making a decision." Those questions are:

- *Will you admire this person?* "If you think about the people you've admired in your life," Bezos explains, "they are probably people you've been able to learn from or take an example from. For myself, I've always tried hard to work only with people I admire, and I encourage folks here to be just as demanding. Life is definitely too short to do otherwise."

- *Will this person raise the average level of effectiveness of the group they're entering?* "We want to fight entropy," Bezos notes. "The bar has to continuously go up. I ask people to visualize the company five years from now. At that point, each of us should look around and say, 'The standards are so high now—boy, I'm glad I got in when I did!' "

- *Will this person bring something extra to the company— some zing, some zip, some lift?* "Many people have unique skills, interests, and perspectives that enrich the work environment for all of us," Bezos says. "It's often something that's not even related to their jobs. One person here is a National Spelling Bee champion. I suspect it doesn't help her in her everyday work, but it does make working here more fun if you can occasionally snag her in the hall with a quick challenge: 'onomatopoeia!' "

Hiring should be a creative and flexible process. A bureaucratic approach may be fine if you're looking for bureaucrats, but not if you are building a nimble corporation. You want people who are well rounded, curious, and involved.

Advertising wizard Arthur Einstein has developed a highly creative "people-picking formula," in which he studies the candidates' head, hands, and shoulders. Each body part represents certain skills or talents. The head, unsurprisingly, is shorthand for the person's intelligence in general, and business savvy in particular. The hands measure skills. Are his abilities restricted to those required for the job, or can she grow and add new skills to the company's mix? Einstein looks at the shoulders to assess how much responsibility a person can carry. The more Einstein can delegate, the more the employee can transcend the boundaries of her original job. Einstein's system is quirky—and, yes, his is a highly creative industry—but the point is to develop a hiring process that is tailored to your company's unique needs. Beware consultants who want to sell you some "foolproof" system that worked for the other guy. You aren't the other guy.

And remember, the hiring process isn't over when the position is offered and accepted. In fact, the period shortly thereafter, when the employee is integrated into the company, is perhaps even more critical. James E. Copeland, Jr., CEO of Deloitte Touche Tohmatsu, believes a manager has to "to turn loose the reins" and let new hires find their sea legs and perform. Copeland observes that "historically, we thought of people as a cost element, and today you have to change that mindset and value them as revenue sources and as intellectual capital. . . . And . . . very carefully pick those areas where you are going to be involved." In other words, experienced managers know how to facilitate their employees' independence, enable them to work creatively, then, stay out of their way.

All of the challenges and solutions I have described above are based on the premise that there is *nothing* more important to a company's success than loyal and talented people.

< MIX WINNERS WITH WINNERS >

It's obvious that hiring superb people makes an organization run smoothly, but less obvious is the dynamic at work. *Winners want to be with winners.* At Lycos, good employees helped us recruit their equals. Instead of the envy and jealousy that you might expect in a highly competitive workplace, these peer-directed people thrived on collaboration. I have found that most talented employees prefer to be players on a winning team, rather than stars on a mediocre one.

I was astounded to hear from Kurt Melden, chief technology officer of Unisphere Networks and a founder of Cascade Communications, that his 750-person company has less than a 2 percent employee turnover per year in an incredibly tight labor market. They only hire the best, he explained, and the strength of the team acts as a talent magnet and bolsters everyone's confidence in success.

It's similar to what you find with a winning sports franchise. The best players want to be there because they believe they can win the championship. Why is it that the New York Yankees have been able to win so many titles? Sure they're a well-funded major market team, but as much as anything, free agents are drawn to the prospects of winning. The same principle applies in the work force.

One of our engineering executives taught me a great term for setting hiring standards: "three-sigma quality." It means that every person on his team should be three standard deviations above the mean. I love the phrase and its implication, and have used it ever since to visualize and articulate outstanding hiring practices.

While it's easy to agree with the idea of recruiting only the best, doing so can be a challenge for many managers. How exactly do you identify the best and brightest? Many criteria must be met before a potential employee qualifies as a "three sigma," but none supersedes character. Jeff Christian, CEO of the executive search firm Christian & Timbers, stressed this point during our preparatory discussions for a search he was conducting for us. He explained that, "more than any other element, we need to find a match with human qualities. The basic skills can be replicated," he said, "the people element cannot." Jeff has been responsible for scores of high-profile placements over the last few years, including Carly Fiorina at Hewlett-Packard, and Stratton Sclavos, president and CEO of Network Solutions.

Jeff is famous for his focus on people both as individuals and as members of a team. His firm was a big help at Lycos, always making sure that a candidate's goals were in line with the company's. Like me, he is a big believer in chemistry. A person's personality, temperament, and style are significant factors in how successful he or she can be. We have all hired a new employee only to realize, usually within days, that the fit is wrong. As previously mentioned, in my haste to build a staff at Lycos, I hired a vice president of marketing without considering our chemistry. Almost immediately, I knew we couldn't get along. I fired him within a few months, but it cost me time, energy, and money.

I learned a lot from that bad hire. Having a discordant note brought down the whole symphony. I was unhappy, my being unhappy had a ripple effect, and there was a subtle but perceptible drop in morale. That's something winning companies, like winning baseball teams, can ill afford.

<INSPIRE YOUR HIRES>

Once you've hired great performers, how do you keep them? Won't they be tempted to explore enticing opportunities elsewhere? The greener-pastures syndrome can often be exacerbated by a company's success. What was once your wonderful start-up, communal and entrepreneurial, has suddenly become big and bureaucratic, bogged down with rules and procedures. But some rules should never change, and the first is treating people fairly and with respect.

You can't expect everyone to agree with each of your decisions, but if all feel that you are fair, you have accomplished a vital part of your job. You won't be able to hold onto good people, no matter how much you pay them, if you don't treat them fairly. Period.

Many of the earlier employees at Lycos were indispensable to our continued growth. The were risk takers who came aboard a small company that had no guarantee of surviving. Their energy and optimism fueled our success. If they had lost their enthusiasm, we might well have stopped moving—like a racing sloop becalmed in a windless sea.

Our challenge was to keep them fired up, passionate, and entrepreneurial. It was never easy, and we didn't always get it right, but we certainly gave it a lot of attention. We emphasized empowerment, product teams, and outside-the-box structure. Lycos Labs was one small program we built to inspire such thinking. It was our playground, a place to experiment freely. It welcomed anyone's ideas for an online enterprise. Lycos funded the lab, acting as a shareholder outside our corporate structure. We provided facilities, computing, accounting, and anything else a start-up needed to get off the ground. The entrepreneurs became employees of their new entity and were considered members of the Lycos community, but with few of its strings attached.

The Lycos Labs concept may not be appropriate for all companies. The point is that there is no one right way to motivate your best people, Of course money plays a role, but most of all, people want to be engaged and inspired. Your employees want to see the results of their labors. They want to feel the impact of their perseverance on the company's success. A rigid organization will never be able to do that.

< DON'T DEMAND LOYALTY—EARN IT>

Machiavelli once said, "You should judge a leader, not by his own qualities, but by those with whom he surrounds himself." I liked to think of myself as a benevolent dictator. I cherished consensus, but I wasn't afraid to let the company know that the buck stopped in my office. I relished making decisions, welcomed top performers, bonded with star players, and never suffered fools gladly. In my view, a business isn't a laboratory for democracy. It's a tough-minded meritocracy that respects winners and has no place for losers.

Having said that, I quickly add that a responsible leader recognizes the fine line between demanding the best and pushing too hard. A manager should have rigorous and tough standards. People should come to work each day prepared to get a job done, and those that don't should feel the heat, while those that do should feel satisfaction and recognition.

At Wang, I worked for a senior executive who constantly belittled and intimidated the people around him. In his mind, everyone from new hires to top managers was equal—equally inferior. He seemed to take pleasure in undermining people's confidence and, apparently, felt bigger when he could make others feel smaller. Naturally, his behavior thwarted creativity, dampened risk-taking, and denied empowerment. Not surprisingly, he led the company toward an abyss and, ultimately, it plunged over. Years later, former Wang executives still remember him bitterly.

A manager can demand excellence, but must earn loyalty. Although employees' allegiance is vital, it's far from automatic. Moreover, it's a two-way street. If managers don't display loyalty, they certainly won't receive it.

Speak to your employees. All of them. I tried hard to talk to every new employee about her or his importance to the success of the company. Once, in a company orientation, I was asked how I could measure whether or not Lycos was a great place to work. My response was that each employee determined it. I said that the ultimate litmus test would be if a close friend called an employee and asked if she should work at the company and, without a moment's hesitation, the employee shouted, "Yes!" Then, and only then, were we a great place to work.

Putting effort into showing people how much they are appreciated is always smart business. All have lives outside of the business—lives that may include ailing parents, young children, marital or financial stress. We ask our employees to put all that aside and come into work every day and give us their best. And if they do, we need to be as loyal as we know how.

A wise employer recognizes that people change—most for the better, some for the worse. Moreover, not every top-notch candidate can deliver on his or her promise. Inevitably, some individuals just can't get the job done, for whatever reason.

How should you deal with talented people who aren't performing? In my view, too many companies flinch at the obvious response. Uncomfortable with tough decisions, managers react by what I call "shaking the canary cage." Nonperformers aren't fired, just reassigned, so you end up with the same canaries on different perches, singing the same sad song.

A strong organization recognizes people who get the job done—and those who don't. You need the courage to confront a poor performer, detail his or her shortcomings, and devise a plan to correct them. And the clear implication must be: Change or move on. Incompetence can't be tolerated; it is no less contagious than competence. If it infects a key process, it can bring down the whole company.

During my interview with John Chambers for the position of regional manager at Wang, he asked me if I could hire a friend. I said, "Of course." Without missing a beat, he fired back, "Could you fire one?" He made his point: Leadership makes the tough calls, and knows that laggards drag down the whole enterprise.

Just as it's important to recognize that good people change, so, too, do good companies. Indeed, they must evolve and adapt to survive. And as that happens they sometimes leave what was once the right person in what is now the wrong job. Perhaps a veteran of the start-up crew—with whom you lived around the clock in the halcyon days of the company's birth—no longer fits in. Unfortunately, a company can't afford to keep formerly great employees. Of course, it may be a matter of finding where they fit in the new model. This is where having knowledge of the person's skills is essential for both of you. Helping people help themselves is one of the greatest satisfactions of authority.

<MAKE PEOPLE BELIEVE THEY ARE WINNERS>

Leadership isn't about telling people what to do. It's about helping them figure out what they're good at—and then inspiring
them to be *great* at it. The goal is employees who believe in
themselves, and use the organization as the arena for expressing their confidence and skill. I agree with Dee Hock, founder
and chief executive officer emeritus of Visa International, when
he says that "given the right circumstances, from no more than
dreams, determination, and the liberty to try, ordinary people
consistently do extraordinary things. To lead is to create those
circumstances."

People who claim they can't do something are invariably
right. You want your people to say and believe that they can meet
a challenge. Having confidence that you'll win is the only way to
get through a crunch, whether you're running a marathon or starting a company. The Ecuadorian philosopher José Ortegay Gasset
once wrote that the way to look at life is through the eyes of a ship-
wrecked sailor—cool, fearless, and absolutely convinced he'll make it.

How do you inculcate this confidence in your employees?
For one thing, get them deeply involved in the company's fate
and fortunes. Not so long ago, an us-versus-them atmosphere
ruled in business. Today, even in heavily unionized industries,
that approach is seen as counterproductive. You want every single person working for you to have a sense of ownership, a feeling that their personal fulfillment is linked to the company's
success. Be open with employees, help them to understand what
you're trying to accomplish. And don't erect any unnecessary barriers between management and employees.

Herb Kelleher encourages open conversation among employees and management. "We're not afraid to talk to our people
about important philosophical . . . things that are . . . perhaps in-
spirational in nature. Our current signature line is that Southwest Airlines is the symbol of freedom. It's not just for the

outside world. It's directed towards telling our people, 'Hey, what you're doing every day is important to millions of people across the U.S. who would not be able to fly.' So you're doing a great amount of good for society."

Recognize people's thirst for information and their desire to feel a part of something bigger than themselves—and make sure to quench it with facts, inspiration, and leadership.

Dick Orlando, a sales executive at Wang, taught me a concept I've come to believe in strongly: overcommunicating. It means that managers should listen closely, keep everyone in the loop, and speak in as direct a manner as possible. Say it, say it again, then say it one more time.

During any period of turmoil, rumors run rampant. At Lycos, it happened during our attempted merger with USA, and again after our actual merger with Terra. During these times, a leader needs to deliver the facts—fast and emphatically. I spent a lot of time emphasizing to managers that they had to constantly communicate our mission, strategy, objectives, and tactics. In turbulent times, I and every manager in the company had a most basic obligation to employees—to keep them informed.

Although the context of the following memo was not our mergers, but rather the stock market declines in spring 2000, it exemplifies what I mean about keeping lines of communication open, especially in a crisis. As you will see, I didn't have a lot of factual information to convey; rather, I wanted all of my employees to know how much I appreciated their hard work, and that I remained optimistic in the face of the current dilemma. It was sent prior to our Terra merger, at the beginning of the NASDAQ collapse.

> 04/19/2000 10:09 AM
>
> To: Lycos Employees
>
> From: Bob Davis
>
> Subject: The market

"It was the best of times, it was the worst of times." What better way to describe the robust growth Lycos continues to enjoy as financial markets declined over the last few weeks. As little as a month ago, the suggestion that the NASDAQ might lose 25 percent of its value in a single week would have been considered absurd. Yet, that is just what happened last week.

So what's going on? I wish had a simple answer. I wish anybody had a simple answer. There is no way to sugar coat the recent declines, but, in a world where misery loves company, we have a lot of companions. As of mid-day Monday, Lycos has actually been one of the best performers during this market pullback.

With that said, and since I can't identify the root causes of the market declines, let me touch on a few related topics. First, Lycos has never been stronger. At no time in our company's history have we been positioned as well . . . We are profitable, enjoying rapid growth in our operating margins, have a stronger and more robust set of products than ever before, and have a winning multi-brand strategy. We have completed the public offering of Lycos Europe, and have four joint ventures preparing for their own IPOs in markets from Singapore to Canada. Lycos was just labeled a *Forbes* 500 company; it has a larger revenue backlog than at any previous time, and has cash and securities worth over $2.5 billion. In short, we are well on our way to becoming a media power-house and blue chip investment.

This pullback will only hasten the consolidation that we have been witnessing in our industry. For a number of reasons, it should become easier for Lycos to acquire businesses. Since we were less adversely affected than so many others, many public companies have become cheaper for us to acquire on a relative basis. Next, we are likely to see far fewer IPOs in the United States over the next several months and those that do get out will be at reduced valuations. Those two factors will cause venture-backed valuations to drop. The bottom line is that there is likely to be trouble ahead for a lot of smaller Internet companies, probably for more than most now realize. Some will surely make it through this period, others will be sold, and many more will just fade away. It is a pattern that has repeated itself in virtually every market consolidation in history. The strong get stronger and, as a leader, we intend to put these conditions to work in our favor.

And finally, the breadth and depth of the market correction is likely to help us on the way back up. It has happened before. In the summer of 1996, Lycos fell by 69 percent only to break through new highs in the succeeding months. I suspect we may see a similar flight toward quality over the next few months; that investors will place their bets on companies with proven business models and solid earnings, such as Lycos. This makes me feel very good about all the hard work you have done to build our company and make it profitable, and I hope it makes you feel good as well. It has surely been a wild few weeks, but don't let this market craziness make you lose sight of just how good we really are. Thanks for your efforts in getting us here, be patient with the markets, maintain your passion, and the future can be ours.

After I sent the memo, I could practically hear the organization breathe a collective sigh of relief. It was all about communication, letting people know I understood their concerns, and inspiring them to forge on.

One-way communication, however, is by definition limited. So, in addition to our monologues, we need to develop ongoing dialogue. Feedback and input are something that we need to aggressively solicit.

A lot of leaders have an intellectual understanding of the importance of feedback, but feel uncomfortable actually listening to it—and that discomfort is invariably communicated non-verbally. Your words may be welcoming, but your tone of voice and body language can reveal your displeasure and, in effect, inhibit or completely block conversation. Realizing the power of unconscious communication, John Seely Brown, chief scientist at Xerox, videotapes his weekly executive meetings so he can study his behavior and see for himself if he is emitting subliminal messages. Then, he works to curb them.

Finally, put some thought into what inspires you. The great comedy writer Neil Simon said that when he writes his plays, he tries to make himself laugh. If something or someone has inspired you, there's a very good chance it will have the same effect on others.

<BUILD A BENCH>

No CEO has been more conscientious in planning his succession than Jack Welch. And he's had a lot of superb candidates to choose from. One reason for GE's extraordinary line of leaders is its Management Development Institute, referred to as "the Harvard of corporate America." The program is well funded, thorough, and—not surprisingly—several of its "graduates" are running other companies. Jeffrey Immelt won the contest to succeed Welch, but the two other primary candidates didn't do too badly—one now runs Home Depot and the other runs 3M.

Welch understands that you have to create challenges within the company that act as incentives for promising managers. Really good people tend to be ambitious, restless, in serious competition with *themselves.* If you can't keep them growing, they'll move to a company that can.

At Lycos, I am proud of the management-development program we created. All managers were required to attend eight days of classroom training over the course of a year. Many of our new first-level managers hadn't yet coped with crises, conflicts, coaching, and counseling. So, we put them through managerial boot camp, and it became an invaluable program.

Managers loved it because it reflected a strong corporate commitment to their careers; employees loved it because their bosses became more effective and understanding; and I loved it because we had a bench that let us identify and develop talent at all levels of the company. If a company is willing to invest in plants, equipment, and infrastructure, isn't it only logical that it invests in its employees?

<CREATE AN EXCEPTIONAL CHALLENGE>

William Jennings Bryant believed that "destiny is not a matter of chance, but a matter of choice. It is not a thing to be waited for, it is a thing to be achieved." Bryant's words have a strong message to leaders and managers: When setting goals for your organization and its people, don't allow mediocrity. Reach for the stars. I liked to think of the objectives I set as "aggressively attainable." Always a little higher than what people thought possible, yet always within the realm of what I thought they could achieve. I agree with Benjamin Zander, conductor of the Boston Philharmonic, who sets as a goal "the maximum capacity that people have"—and settles for no less. He sees himself as "a relentless architect of the possibilities of human beings."

We tried to reach for those ideals at Lycos. In August 1999, we decided that we were going to generate 165 million page views per day over the next year. At the time, we were getting 50 million viewings per day. The new goal was excessive, and we realized that, but we also saw it as a rallying cry for the company. We became absolutely determined to build or buy our way to our goal. We plastered the building with billboards saying "165 Million Or Bust!" And what happened? By July 2000, we ended up achieving 201 million page-viewings per day—far more than even our extraordinary expectation.

The lesson is that an exceptional challenge can motivate a company to reach extraordinary heights. It creates a sense of common purpose, along with that powerful motivator—a common enemy. Who in the market are we determined to beat?

Jeff Bezos tells prospective employees that they will work long, hard, and smart; but "at Amazon.com, you can't choose two out of three." Building an institution "that matters to our customers...that we can all tell our grandchildren about is not meant to be easy." Leo Burnett, who founded the advertising agency Leo Burnett and Partners, puts it wonderfully: "When you reach for the stars, you may not quite get one, but you won't come up with a handful of mud either."

Give your team an exceptional challenge and watch it rise to the occasion. More than financial reward, I think the true secret to building a company is to create the feeling that your team is undertaking an incredible mission and will—against all odds—succeed. Robert Browning said that "our aspirations are our possibilities." In December of 2000, Lycos had 350 million page-viewings a day to prove it.

If you analyze any of the great companies over the last hundred years, you'll find that they that were all built on a foundation of people. Many started because of a powerful idea or new technology, but that's never been enough to sustain greatness. Because for all of our wondrous technology, in the end it all comes down to us.

EPILOGUE

AS THE FOUNDER OF THE FIRST truly global Internet media company, I was lucky enough to be a part of history. Not that I realized it at all at the time. A decade ago only a handful of people were prescient enough to envision the impact of this remarkable new medium. Today, just about everyone recognizes that the Internet is one of the most revolutionary developments ever conceived by the human mind. Even as you read this, it is rewriting the rules of commerce and communication.

Clearly, the Internet is not only a key player in the future, it is actually *creating* that future. You have the power to determine how that future plays out for your own business. That is a significant responsibility and a thrilling challenge.

This book has detailed some of my hard-won business experience, the trials and errors, and, yes, the triumphs. It's a dispatch from the front lines. I'm mainly speaking to businesspeople, but the Internet is much more than a business tool. It is having a profound effect on politics, medicine, education, the arts; in fact every aspect of life in every corner of the globe is being altered by the Internet's ability to link people, process data, and provide information.

At this point in the Internet revolution, hardly anyone doubts its power. And it has all happened in what history will record as the blink of an eye. Five years ago, the Internet had

13 million users, a mere drop in the global bucket. As I write this, it connects 350 million people. Half the world's inhabitants have never made a telephone call, yet Internet traffic doubles every 100 days. In another four years, according to *The Economist*, the total number of users will exceed 1 billion.

Economically, the Internet creates opportunities for people who might otherwise never enter the business world; politically, it has helped blur national boundaries; socially, it has diminished distinctions based on age, gender, and race.

But Internet misconceptions still abound. Though some call it an industry, I believe it is actually a medium of communication, not unlike a telephone line. It is a medium that is driving the growth of thousands of businesses across dozens of industries. The companies that exist on it and provide its services often have no more in common than, well, the medium itself. Trying to compare Lycos with Amazon.com, or Cisco with Yahoo!, or Intel with America Online, is as meaningless as comparing General Motors with Procter & Gamble. Although GM and P&G are both manufacturers, they are in very different in just about every other way.

The Internet owes its existence to the expanding capacity of silicon chips. As Gordon Moore, co-founder of Intel, noted in 1965, chips shrink by half and double their information-handling ability every 18 months. This phenomenon, widely known as Moore's Law, shows no indication of slowing down.

This expanding capacity drives costs down and productivity up. Computers have become ubiquitous: Their global power has multiplied a billion times in 40 years. Today's Ford Taurus contains more computing power than all the mainframe computers used in the Apollo space program. Oil drillers using seismic-exploration technology have reduced the cost of finding oil from nearly $10 a barrel in 1991 to a dollar today. Without silicon chips, we could be paying $40 a barrel for oil instead of the $30 we grumble about. Low-cost e-mail shrinks the world and e-commerce has created a global shopping mall. Business Web sites transform the communications, technology, logistics, manufacturing, and management style of the global economy.

The Internet differs from previous technological breakthroughs. The cost savings, for example, are far more dramatic. Computing costs have fallen by an average of 35 percent annually for the past 30 years. No other innovation has shown such sustainable efficiencies.

Accordingly, computers and the Internet are being adopted far more quickly than previous technologies. It took 90 years for electricity to go from invention to powering half of U.S. industry, but the Internet reaches 50 percent of U.S. households less than six years after its commercialization. The Internet also promises to be the first technology to increase productivity in services, which now comprise 60 percent of America's total output.

But to be sure, the Internet has ample room to grow: Only 6 percent of the world's population is online. Technologies are always slow to spread in their early years, but they mushroom when a critical mass is achieved—and the evidence suggests that the Internet will soon reach that point. It is estimated that by 2003 60 percent of the U.S. population online and worldwide e-commerce revenues in 2003 should reach $1.4 trillion.

And so I'm disturbed by the disparaging attitude and comments toward the Internet that have lately been emanating from some quarters. I think it's important for those of us in the business community to recognize the difference between market economics, irrational exuberance, and the underlying technology.

The explosive growth in the price of technology stocks that we witnessed on the NASDAQ over the last five years was a once-in-a-lifetime phenomenon. It really was the twentieth century's gold rush. And any student of history can tell you that the California gold rush bred behavior that can be classified as illogical, foolish, and even crazy. A true mania took hold, both in the foothills of the Sierra Nevadas and on the stock exchanges. And in both cases, some people got very rich and a lot of people ended up losing a lot of money.

I don't get any pleasure from being tough on those investors who paid hundreds of dollars for one share of stock in an Internet company that not only had no profits, but no revenues. We all want to make as much money as we can, but greed is an emotion, and emotions can sometimes overwhelm the intellect and lead us to make irrational decisions.

But belief in the Internet itself is not only rational, it's imperative. This is a world-changing medium and its impact will only continue to grow. Those Internet companies that are built on a solid, sustainable vision and model are thriving. The failure of those companies based on nothing but a catchy name with a ".com" on the end of it is hardly surprising. Those companies never had a chance to begin with. My confidence in the Internet has never been stronger.

So, as Internet stocks continue their wild ride, I sometimes think of that wise and wonderful poem by Rudyard Kipling, "If," that begins: "If you can keep your head when all about you are losing theirs . . ." Now is the time to keep our heads and not lose our faith in one of the most wondrous developments in human history. That is not to say we will ever return to the sense of irrational euphoria as it relates to many dot-com valuations. But we should surely not confuse a very small number of companies that rode a bubble with the profound change this medium will have on all of us.

It should be obvious by now that I'm in awe of the Internet and grateful that I was able to play a small part in its early history. It has been a profoundly fulfilling experience.

As January 2000 drew to a close, therefore, I felt as if I were on top of the world. Lycos was in great shape. Revenues were soaring, earnings were up, and the company had just reported financial results that, for the sixteenth consecutive quarter, topped Wall Street's expectations. Best of all, having just completed an extremely successful secondary offering of almost 6 million shares of common stock, we were sitting on a war chest of over $600 million in cash. I especially liked the way one online columnist summed up our position: "After a fall run-up and a surge Wednesday in the wake of a Q2 earnings report that exceeded analysts' expectations, Lycos is hot again."

The company was strong and the NASDAQ was soaring. The combination made it the perfect time to sell the business.

As you know, I've always been a fervent believer in the Internet economy, but it was clear at that juncture that valuations of many Internet companies had reached stratospheric levels. Any student of economics would have told us that they simply weren't sustainable. How could Yahoo!, even considering all its earnings, audience, and momentum, be worth more than Disney and CBS combined? Maybe someday, but surely not in January 2000. In fact, for a company that executed well on so many fronts, I suspect Yahoo!'s failure to use its $130 billion-plus market cap to create a transforming event will be looked back upon as one of the greatest missed business opportunities of all time. Yahoo! could have purchased virtually any business it chose, yet its determination to remain pure to an Internet-only model deprived the company of the chance to build scale on a grand dimension. Only time will tell, but I believe the company left a massive opportunity on the table and will ultimately be owned by one of the old-economy companies it should have acquired. So as much as I was enjoying every minute of every day, it was the perfect time to lock in a great return for our shareholders and close the Lycos story.

Another advantage of selling was that we didn't *need* to sell. It is always best to negotiate from a position of strength. I had the luxury of being able to walk away from any suitor. We were calling the shots and our requirements were straightforward. We would sell Lycos if, and only if, we could receive a significant premium for our shareholders and, even more important, we could structure what I termed a "transformative event": That is, a combination that would alter the competitive landscape and position the resultant company as a powerful force for years to come.

This last factor was critical to me for a number of reasons.

First, I was very proud of what we had built and was only interested in a transaction that would maintain the Lycos legacy. We had become a household name around the world, and I felt that heritage should last a lifetime. Second, I felt a strong obligation to both our shareholders and to the sell-side research analysts who had supported us over the years. In the wake of the failed USA merger, any deal needed to offer an instant financial premium for those who elected to "cash out," as well as a secure long-term vehicle for those who hoped to continue investing in the company. Finally, and high on my list, was my commitment to the well-being of the employees. They made the company successful, and I felt extremely loyal to them.

Yes, I had quite a demanding wish list, but I was in the catbird's seat. There were only two independent global portals remaining in the market. Yahoo!, with hefty valuation, was one. We were the other. I was just waiting for the right the knock on the door.

Paul Haigney, of the investment-banking firm Lazard Frères, first introduced me to Terra Networks. We had quite a history with Paul, who, when he was at Wasserstein Perella, represented Lycos in the USA transaction. I always believed he felt a sense of guilt, undeservedly so, for our failure to get that deal done, and as a result worked doubly hard to restore our good graces. A knowledgeable and competent person, he often phoned me with good ideas.

One day Paul called to tell me that he was working with Telefónica, the Spanish telecommunications giant and parent company to Terra Networks. Terra Networks had built a great franchise as the dominant portal and Internet service provider for the Spanish-speaking world—a population of some 550 million—and now it was interested in acquiring Lycos. The company's success had been rewarded with a very robust market value. Nonetheless, I told Paul I wasn't interested. I just didn't see the combination resulting in a transformative event. Paul deferred to my judgment.

But that wasn't the end of it. Soon afterward he phoned

again, this time to suggest a joint Latin American venture with Terra. I agreed to discuss it, and a few days later I welcomed Terra's CFO to our Boston offices. It was a short meeting.

Within 15 minutes it became clear that Terra had no real interest in a joint venture; the actual purpose of the visit was to discuss an acquisition. Paul apologized for the surprise, I walked out, and our first meeting ended somewhat less than warmly.

Not ones to give up easily, the Terra team came back at us yet again. This time they suggested that they had the basis for my transformative event: Telefónica was willing to step to the table and contribute certain of its assets to the new enterprise. After some discussion, I agreed to a meeting in Miami with Terra's CEO, Abel Linares, and Telefónica's chairman, Juan Villalonga, on one side of the table and Ted Philip and me on the other.

We spent the better part of a Friday posturing and positioning until it became clear that their bid and our expectations were very far apart. We resumed negotiations on Monday with Juan presenting a substantially improved offer, but once again it fell well short of our requirements. At the end of the day, everyone agreed that we were too far apart to expect a deal, and we terminated our discussions on good terms.

Ted and I flew back to Boston with Juan and Abel aboard Telefónica's Gulfstream IV, before it continued on to Spain. During the flight the four of us engaged in informal, more personal discussions and I realized how closely our visions for a global market aligned. When we deplaned in Boston, both Ted and I commented on how impressed we were and much we liked the whole Telefónica and Terra teams.

All was quiet for several weeks, and then I received a call from Thomas Middelhoff, who you may recall is the chairman of the German media titan, Bertelsmann. The call itself was a clear demonstration of how global our markets have become; I received it on my cell phone in Amsterdam from my German partner who was working from his New York office. Thomas had been working successfully with Telefónica on other matters and had heard rumors of our merger discussions. He explained that the then pending AOL–Time Warner combination left him in a quandary. He had been a longtime member of the AOL board and had developed much of his Internet strategy around that relationship. The proposed merger of AOL with his long-standing rival Time Warner risked leaving him without a vehicle to implement his Internet strategy. He was interested in exploring what a Terra-Lycos-Telefónica-Bertelsmann alliance might look like. After much conversation, we agreed that he would broker a meeting in Miami the following week between the four companies.

A few days later, Thomas and I flew from New York to Miami aboard a Bertelsmann-chartered Learjet to begin our dialogue anew. With the aborted USA deal in the front of my mind, I had no interest in any arrangement that wasn't a clear victory for Lycos, although that is not to say a victory for Lycos alone. I envisioned the acquirer winning as well. Accordingly, I began the meeting by explaining what I meant by a market-transforming event: one that altered the competitive landscape by positioning the combined enterprise to become the twenty-first century's dominant online media company. By the end of the day, we were all on the same page.

After many tense moments and two or three weeks of hard negotiations, we had our deal. On May 15, 2000, we announced the agreement. First, Lycos shareholders would receive a premium of more than 100 percent over our then current stock price. And, due to shrewd advice from one of the nation's best merger-and-acquisition minds, Ethan Topper, of Credit Suisse First Boston, we insisted on a collar that protected the premium by shielding Lycos shareholders from any drop in Terra price by as much as 20 percent. Given the NASDAQ decline that summer, this clause ended up being worth over $1 billion in the deal price.

Another term, which at times came close to being a deal breaker, was my insistence that we provide some form of accelerated vesting for all employees. Terra was willing to offer this to the senior management team, but steadfastly refused any acceleration for employees at large. They argued that options were a necessary motivation if employees were going to stay with the company after the merger. Their position was certainly understandable, but Ted and I felt passionately about this point and refused to accept any deal that didn't provide an immediate benefit, beyond the premium, to the hundreds of men and women who had helped build Lycos. Furthermore, we knew that if meaningful bonds were going to develop in the new company, they would have to be based on loyalty and commitment. Ultimately, they relented, and each employee was vested for an additional 12 months. This translated into many millions of dollars for our employees.

The contributions of Telefónica and Bertelsmann addressed my need to change the competitive landscape. Telefónica agreed to subscribe in full to a rights offering that would provide the combined company with $2 billion in cash, in addition to the $1 billion we already had. With $3 billion, our company would become one of the most highly capitalized in the world. In fact, if we were a Fortune 50 company, we would have ranked twenty-third in cash on hand. Telefónica also agreed to contribute all of its wireless Internet business to a new joint venture we would call Terra Moviles. We would own approximately 50 percent of this new entity and, with it, we would have a platform for the delivery of our content in the rapidly emerging wireless world. With over 23 million subscribers, Telefónica is one of the largest wireless providers on the planet and offered expertise in this market that would have taken us years to develop.

Bertelsmann's contributions were equally significant. First, it agreed to a five-year, $1 billion online advertising buy. At a time when Internet advertising was under pressure, this was the largest contract in the history of the industry. Perhaps even more important, Bertelsmann granted us access to distribute certain of its media properties on the Internet. In an age of convergence, this was a priceless benefit.

One of the final and more difficult points to resolve was how the resulting company would be managed. Though I was excited about the merger, I wasn't interested in staying on unless the Lycos management team, in whom I had complete confidence, and I would be running the new company. For days,

Villalonga tried to convince me to take a different role and stressed that Terra needed to appoint the CEO. He was equally clear that he feared that the combined company would suffer if I were to leave altogether, and he wouldn't go forward if this was the case. I refused to budge. At the eleventh hour, as the deal was close to falling apart, Juan agreed to my terms. I would become CEO, Ted Philip would be our chief financial officer, and Terra CEO Abel Linares would become chief operating officer of the new company, which we were naming Terra Lycos.

We had our transforming event, an exceptional premium for our shareholders, and, even though it was Lycos that was being acquired, we retained management control of Terra Lycos.

The progress of the merger was widely reported prior to the official announcement, and, in response, Lycos' stock price was soaring. Someone was leaking the news. We held most of the final negotiations at Wachtell Lipton Rosen & Katz, Terra's New York counsel, whose building overflowed with our collective personnel. One of the many bankers, lawyers, accountants, and employees of Terra or Lycos managed to feed nearly every detail of our merger to the *New York Times*. It was an amazing saga. We would negotiate through the night, then read about it in the morning paper. I was afraid that the actual announcement would be anticlimactic.

Not surprisingly though, our public-relations team handled the advance reports masterfully. It was a top-notch group that, in addition to our own extremely competent employees, included Paul Costello, former press secretary for First Lady Rosalynn Carter and now with the New York public-relations firm of Shandwick Miller; and George Sard, president of the leading New York investor- and financial-advisory firm, Sard Verbinnen.

We scheduled a press conference for 4:30 P.M. on May 16. As I sat in Villalonga's suite at the Four Seasons hotel signing the merger documents, the Equitable Auditorium, which we had rented for the event, was filling up with media, shareholders, and employees. A short time later, Thomas Middelhoff, Villalonga, and I stood before a packed house and outlined our vision for Terra Lycos. We had completed the Web's first international merger and would have a presence in 40 countries. Our $3 billion in cash made us the world's best-financed Internet company, and we were backed by global giants in both the telecommunications and media industries. I could not have been happier and was thrilled when, as I began speaking from the podium, I saw a standing ovation take hold in the crowd.

I knew, however, that I might have one more issue to contend with. Dave Wetherell still held about 15 percent of the company's stock. Given our history, I was concerned about his public reaction to the merger, but when I informed him, which I did in advance of the press conference moments after the market closed, he was most gracious and congratulated me on a "brilliantly architectured" deal. He reiterated those comments the next evening on CNBC, and I felt that everything was going well. A few days later, I brought Dave and Juan together with the hope of securing a public declaration from Dave that he planned to vote in favor of the merger. Also, I felt it might be time to mend fences and in that spirit I planned to discuss how Telefónica or Terra Lycos could work with CMGI or its companies. Dave gave us a 90-minute overview of his portfolio, at the end of which Juan asked the billion-dollar question: "Can we count on your public support?" I was appalled by his reply. We would receive it, Dave answered, if we met one of three sets of criteria:

1. Terra Lycos purchased at least $300 million in services from CMGI over three years;
2. Terra Lycos purchased a total of $150 million in shares from four different CMGI companies; or
3. Telefónica or Terra purchased CMGI's shares of Lycos for $90 a share. At the time, Lycos was trading at approximately $55 a share and CMGI held about 14 million shares.

Once again, I felt our interests were betrayed as Dave attempted to leverage our success into CMGI's benefit. It was clear I was in for a long summer. But CMGI, it turned out, was to be the least of my worries. Juan Villalonga had run into political problems back home over his expansionist views and a failed merger attempt with the Dutch telecommunications company KPN. His global ambitions risked diluting Spanish ownership of the previously state-owned telephone company, which he had helped to privatize. In midsummer, amid a storm of controversy and under intense pressure from numerous factions in Spain, Villalonga resigned his post. I had a terrible sense of déjà vu and, once again, the question became "Will the deal go through?" As the combination of CMGI's silence and Telefónica's turmoil introduced that very ugly element of uncertainty.

Fortunately, Telefónica quickly named a new chairman, César Alierta, who promptly announced his support for our merger. But, just as quickly, to my disappointment and surprise, he named longtime GE veteran Joaquim Agut as Terra's Executive Chairman, a position held in title only by Villalonga. I would now have a full-time boss when the merger closed. When I questioned the decision, Alierta said that he needed a Spanish executive to look after Telefónica's interests.

I understood his position. After all, he didn't know me, and was in the process of spending billions for our company. My objections were moot at that point anyway—the decision had been made and announced. My issue, to be clear, was never with Agut. I didn't know the man. My issue was that I had negotiated long and hard for control of the business and saw that agreement collapse before my eyes. I hoped otherwise, but feared that the role I had planned for myself might never materialize.

While all of this was going on, I went back to Dave Wetherell numerous times seeking his public support. After all, I argued, announcing that you will be voting for the merger will help CMGI, Lycos, and our other stakeholders. He refused, saying he needed to keep his options open. In his defense, Dave did publicly state that he liked the deal. What he wouldn't state publicly is that he would vote for it. Ted and I couldn't avoid the issue. We must have been asked a thousand times, by the press, shareholders, and other interested parties, how CMGI would vote. I always expressed optimism, but I could never offer the certainty that the market was asking for.

Meanwhile, the months passed. It was now early October and our shareholder vote was under way. We had mailed the proxy in late September and scheduled the shareholder meeting for a month later. The votes had started to come in, and they were overwhelmingly in favor of the deal, including CMGI's. I called Wetherell to thank him and ask him to issue a press release stating how he had voted. Though he refused, he agreed to my counterproposal that Lycos issue a release to this effect and, on October 9, we told the markets that CMGI had voted all of its shares in favor of the merger.

On October 27, 2000, we conducted our shareholder meeting and proudly announced that 99.4 percent of votes cast were in favor of the merger. It was a landslide. We had sold Lycos, the company that we built from just $2 million in venture funding, for over $5.4 billion. This represents a return on that initial $2 million we received from CMGI of over 269,900 percent in a little over five years.

Despite the euphoria of the numbers, it was a also melancholy day. I felt pride and jubilation in completing the sale, but as the congratulations poured in I couldn't help but feel saddened that our company, as we knew it, no longer existed.

As the weeks passed I became increasingly sure that it was time for me to move on. Terra Lycos remained a potent force, perhaps even more so than I had initially envisioned. The company's quarterly results, released in February 2001, showed dramatic growth at a time when most of its competitors were stumbling. The issue for me, however, related to day-to-day management of the company.

Since 1995 I had run Lycos and had enjoyed every minute of it. I felt the freedom to steer the business into the tailwinds of some great successes and the headwinds of some tough disappointments. Under the new structure, it was clear that I would no longer be at the controls. I raised these concerns with my new partners and was encouraged by their expressed desire to have me share power with Agut. By this time we'd developed a solid working relationship and I respected both his intelligence and business acumen. The reality, though, is that very few companies can succeed with two masters. It wouldn't have been good for me, Agut, or Terra Lycos. On February 1, 2001, I resigned as the CEO of Terra Lycos.

But walking away from Terra Lycos completely was not something I had any desire to do. So in late January, when outlining to Agut my plans to leave, I was refreshed by his urging that if he could not convince me to stay as an employee that I stay in another capacity. I agreed to become the vice chairman of the company's board of directors and remain on the boards of each of our worldwide joint ventures. In this way, I'll have the time to pursue my other interests while also supporting the company in a very strategic fashion.

The Lycos experience was a dream come true. In less than six years, we built a worldwide consumer brand and created billions in value. I saw the birth of a medium that has effected more social, political, and economic change than perhaps any other in the history of humankind. The Terra merger left the company in good hands and rewarded those employees and shareholders who had worked so hard to build the business.

Maybe not completely a storybook ending but also not very far from it. Lycos, as a result of the merger, is a stronger company today and is ensured a long-lasting legacy. Terra Lycos is one of the few clear leaders in the still rapidly growing new economy.

And as for me, I have joined my friend Dan Nova as a partner at Highland Capital, one of the nation's leading venture capital firms. In this role, I will have the opportunity to assist and invest in our next generation of entrepreneurs. At the same time, I remain hooked on the adrenaline I find in running a business and will continue to roll up my sleeves, thinking of ways to do it all again.

SOURCES

Speed Is Life is based on my personal recollections. Quotes, anecdotes, or facts from sources other than me or interviews conducted exclusively for this book are listed below.

Chapter 2
SPEED IS LIFE
Source for the quote from Carleton "Carly" S. Fiorina, chairman, chief executive officer, and president, Hewlett-Packard Company: Carleton S. Fiorina, speech, "Art of Reinvention in the New Economy," Chicago, Illinois, April 17, 2000; Carleton S. Fiorina, speech, commencement ceremony, Massachusetts Institute of Technology, June 2, 2000.

Source for the quote from James E. Copeland, Jr., chief executive officer of Deloitte Touche Tohmatsu: "The Challenges for Leaders in the New Economy," *Chief Executive*, August 2000, pages 2 through 5.

Source for the quote from John F. Welch, Jr., chairman and chief executive officer, The General Electric Company: John F. Welch, Lawrence Bossidy, William Weiss, Michael Walsh, and Stratford Sherman, "A Master Class in Radical Change," *Fortune*, December 13, 1993, page 82.

Source for the quote from Kevin Kelley, editor, *Wired* magazine: Tom Peters, *The Circle of Innovation* (New York: Alfred A. Knopf, Inc., 1997).

Source for the quote from Warren E. Buffett, chairman and chief executive officer, Berkshire Hathaway, Inc. Janet Lowe, *Warren Buffett Speaks* (New York: John Wiley & Sons, Inc., 1997), page 19.

Source for the quotes from Steven M. Case, chairman, AOL Time Warner, Inc.: Stephen M. Case, speech, Jupiter Communications Annual Conference, New York, New York, March 5, 1998.

Source for the quote from William Gates, chairman, Microsoft Corporation: William Gates, *Business at the Speed of Thought* (New York: Warner Books, 1999).

Chapter 3
YOU LET UP, YOU LOSE
Source for the anecdotes and quotes from Judah Folkman: www.achievement.org.

Source for the anecdotes and quotes from director Ron Howard: www.achievement.org.

Source for the anecdotes and quotes from Sam Donaldson:
www.achievement.org.

Chapter 4
GET BIG FAST
Source for the quote from Carleton "Carly" S. Fiorina, chairman, chief
executive officer, and president, Hewlett-Packard Company: Carleton S.
Fiorina, speech, National Governors Association, Washington, D. C.,
February 27, 2000.

Source for the quotes from Douglas Daft, chairman and chief executive
officer, The Coca-Cola Company: Doug Daft, speech, "Expanding From
Global to Local," British & American Chamber of Commerce, London,
England, May 10, 2000.

Source for the quote from Marc Andreessen, chairman and co-founder of
Loudcloud, Inc.: Gary Andrew Poole, "A Startup's Startup," *Forbes ASAP*,
April 3, 2000, page 111.

Chapter 5
IT'S ALL ABOUT BRAND
Source for the anecdotes and quote from Howard Schultz, chairman and
chief executive officer, Starbucks Corporation: Lori Ioannou, "King Bean,"
Fortune Small Business, 2000.

Source for the quote from Michael Eisner, chairman and chief executive
officer, The Walt Disney Company: "Common Sense and Conflict—An
Interview With Disney's Michael Eisner," *Harvard Business Review*,
January–February 2000, page 114.

Source for the quote from Carleton "Carly" S. Fiorina, chairman, chief
executive officer, and president, Hewlett-Packard Company: Carleton S.
Fiorina, speech, HP Shareholders Meeting, Cupertino, California,
February 29, 2000.

Source for the material on recent problems with Firestone tires: Mark
Magnier, "Bridgestone's Top Man Resigns, a Victim of Firestone Scandal,"
Los Angeles Times, January 12, 2001, part C, page 1.

Source for the material on Johnson & Johnson's problems with Tylenol:
Glen Fest, "Ethics for Employees," *The Fort Worth Star-Telegram*, December
11, 2000.

Source for the quote from Jeffrey P. Bezos, founder, chairman, and
chief executive officer, Amazon. com, Inc.: Jeffrey P. Bezos, "Letter to
Shareholders," *1998 Annual Report*, Amazon.com., Inc.

Source for the quote from Bob Woodward, executive editor, the *Washington Post*: Tony Case, "Woodward Says Journalism Game Has Changed," *Editor & Publisher*, March 11, 1995, page 15.

Chapter 6
PROFIT IS NOT A FOUR-LETTER WORD
Source for the quote from Warren E. Buffett, chairman and chief executive officer, Berkshire Hathaway, Inc. Janet Lowe, *Warren Buffett Speaks* (New York: John Wiley & Sons, Inc., 1997), page 85.

Source for the material on the performance of equity markets in the United States and abroad: Robert J. Shiller, *Irrational Exuberance* (Princeton, New Jersey: Princeton University Press, 2000).

Source for the quote from Melissa Bradley, founder and president, BHC Inc.: Rekha Balu, "Starting Your Startup," *Fast Company*, February 2000.

Chapter 7
BE GREAT AT WHAT YOU'RE GOOD AT
Source for the anecdotes and quotes from Tom Brokaw, anchor and managing editor, NBC Nightly News: Jill Rosenfeld, "Training to Work," *Fast Company*, August 2000.

Source for the anecdote and quote from Leslie H. Wexner, founder and chief executive officer, The Limited, Inc.: Leslie H. Wexner, "Chairman's Letter," *1997 Annual Report*, The Limited, Inc.

Source for the quote from Gerald M. Levin, chief executive officer, AOL Time Warner, Inc.: Gerald M. Levin, speech, "The World on a String," Town Hall, Los Angeles, California, June 11, 1998.

Source for the anecdote and quote from Charles Schwab, chairman and co-chief executive officer, The Charles Schwab Corporation: Nicholas Stein, "How Do You Make the Most Admired List?", *Fortune*, October 2, 2000.

Source for the quote from John F. Welch, Jr., chairman and chief executive officer, The General Electric Company: John F. Welch, Jr., Lawrence Bossidy, William Weiss, Michael Walsh, and Stratford Sherman, "A Master Class in Radical Change," *Fortune*, December 13, 1993, page 82.

Chapter 8
EVERY MOMENT WITH A CUSTOMER IS A MOMENT OF TRUTH
Source for the anecdote and quotes from Herb Kelleher, chairman and chief executive officer, Southwest Airlines Company: "Air Herb's Secret Weapon," *Chief Executive*, July/August 1999, page 32.

Source for the anecdote about The Walt Disney Company: Bill Capodagli and Lynn Jackson, *The Disney Way* (New York: McGraw-Hill, Inc., 1999).

Source for the anecdote and quotes from Stanley Marcus, chairman emeritus of the Neiman Marcus Company: Anna Muoio, "Sales School," *Fast Company*, November 1998.

Source for the anecdotes and quotes from Danny Meyer, president of Union Square Hospitality Group: Lucy McCauley, "How May I Help You?", *Fast Company*, March 2000.

Source for the anecdotes and quotes from Yap Kim Wah, senior vice president of marketing services at Singapore Airlines, Ltd.: Lucy McCauley, "How May I Help You?", *Fast Company*, March 2000.

Chapter 9
PEOPLE ARE YOUR FOUNDATION!
Source for the quote from Carleton "Carly" S. Fiorina, chairman, chief executive officer, and president, Hewlett-Packard Company: Carleton S. Fiorina, speech, commencement ceremony, Massachusetts Institute of Technology, June 2, 2000.

Source for the quote from Albert Einstein: Jerry Mayer and John P. Holms, *Bite-Size Einstein* (New York, New York: St. Martins Press, 1996), page 25.

Source for the anecdote and quotes from Herb Kelleher, chairman and chief executive officer, Southwest Airlines Company: "Air Herb's Secret Weapon," *Chief Executive*, July/August 1999, page 32.

Source for the quotes from Jeffrey P. Bezos, founder, chairman, and chief executive officer, Amazon.com, Inc.: Jeffrey P. Bezos, "Letter to Shareholders," *1998 Annual Report*, Amazon.com., Inc.

Source for the quote and other material from advertising executive Arthur Einstein: Anna Muoio, "The Secrets of Their Success—And Yours," *Fast Company*, issue 9, page 67.

Source for the quotes from James E. Copeland, Jr., chief executive officer, Deloitte Touche Tohmatsu: "The Challenges for Leaders in the New Economy," *Chief Executive*, August 2000, pages 2 through 5.

Source for the quote from Dee W. Hock, founder and chief executive officer emeritus of Visa International, Inc.: "What It Means to Lead," *Fast Company*, February 1997, page 97.

Source for the quote from Benjamin Zander, conductor, Boston Philharmonic: Tom Peters, *The Circle of Innovation* (New York, New York: Alfred A. Knopf, Inc., 1997).

ABOUT THE AUTHOR

Bob Davis was the founder and CEO of Lycos from inception in June 1995, where he completed the fastest IPO in NASDAQ history, a mere nine months from incorporation to offering, through its merger into Terra Lycos in 2001. He continues to serve as the company's Vice Chairman while now working as a partner at the venture capital firm of Highland Capital Partners. Under Bob's leadership, Lycos, with an audience of 91 million people worldwide, has grown from a company with just $2 million in venture capital money into one of the most visited online destinations worldwide and a multi-billion dollar valuation.

He appears regularly on CNN, CNBC, BBC, Bloomberg Radio and TV and has been prominently featured in the *New York Times*, *The Wall Street Journal*, the *Boston Globe*, the *Washington Post*, *Financial Times*, *Forbes*, *Fortune*, *Business Week*, and other major publications. Bob is a frequent speaker and lecturer on the Internet and e-commerce and has addressed numerous industry and civic groups including the U.S. Council on Foreign Relations, the United Nations, the National Press Club, and the United States Congress. He also served as a member of President Bush's technology advisory committee and has advised former President Clinton and former Vice President Gore on matters relating to Internet regulation.

Bob holds a bachelor of science degree, summa cum laude, from Northeastern University and an MBA, with high distinction, from Babson College. He also received an honorary Doctor of Commercial Sciences from Bentley College in May 1999, and an honorary doctorate from Northeastern University in June 2000.

INDEX

www.lycos.com